FOLK BAGS

FOLK BAGS

30 KNITTING PATTERNS & TALES FROM AROUND THE WORLD

VICKI SQUARE

INTERWEAVE PRESS
www.interweave.com

Dedication

To Johnny, my husband and helpmate, for all his love and prayers

———————————

Editor: Amy Goldschlager
Technical editor: Jean Lampe
Illustrations: Vicki Square and Interweave Press, Inc.
Photography: Joe Coca
Photo styling: Ann Swanson
Cover and interior design: Susan Wasinger
Production: Dean Howes
Proofreader: Nancy Arndt

 Interweave Press, Inc.
201 East Fourth Street
Loveland, Colorado 80537-5655 USA
www.interweave.com

Printed in Hong Kong through Phoenix Offset

Library of Congress Cataloging-in-Publication Data

Square, Vicki, 1954-
   Folk bags : 30 knitting patterns and tales from around the world / Vicki Square.
      p. cm.
Includes bibliographical references and index.
   ISBN 1-931499-25-X
   1. Knitting—Patterns. 2. Bags. 3. Handbags. I. Title.
   TT825.S7136 2003
   746.43'2043—dc21
                                        2003006314

10 9 8 7 6 5 4 3 2

Acknowledgments

The credits roll past at the end of a movie, and just like the myriad of people it takes to produce a film, it takes a great team of people to give life to a book. I have been blessed in this respect and have many people to thank for their part in this professional production. Designing this collection of bags and writing this book has been exciting and deeply satisfying. As an artist, I find that when I am completely immersed in the creative process, my reward is the energizing of my entire being.

For making this book a reality, I'm very grateful to Linda Ligon, at the helm of Interweave Press, and her book staff, for believing in me, and for giving me carte blanche on this project from the beginning. Thanks to Betsy Armstrong, my editorial director, who always encouraged me and kept me focused; to Amy Goldschlager, my insightful and thorough content editor, who made sense of my writing and encouraged my personality to shine through; and to Jean Lampe, a technical editorial genius, who has an eye for detail and develops innovative solutions. Thanks to Ann Swanson for her photo stylist's vision, and to photographer extraordinaire Joe Coca, an artist of tremendous talent.

I also extend my gratitude to my knitting colaborers who worked closely with me: Alice Bush, Lois Eynon, Nancy Hewitt, Sheri Kroneberger, Joan Pickett, Elaine Sipes, and Sally Thieszen. I couldn't have done it without you! Thanks to all my Monday night and Thursday afternoon knitters who have been with me for years— you are a constant encouragement. Thanks to Elizabeth Nance, longtime friend and fellow fiber artist, for her inspirations. Thanks to dear friend Caroline Yonker, the handbag queen, for showing me the delight in carrying a different bag every day! And my appreciation goes to all the yarn companies and their representatives who were so gracious in providing yarn for these wonderful projects.

Finally, thank you to my family, husband Johnny and kids Justine and Alex, for allowing me the tunnel vision I needed to do this body of work. They kept the home from falling apart around me while I mananged to ignore just about everything but my work. And that work felt like play, which is truly a gift from God.

Contents

FOLK BAGS

I have always loved art and its history. Given the technological constraints of the time, the achievements of the past were often dramatic and extraordinary. The cache of artistic treasures and the cultural traditions left behind by those bygone artists provoke our admiration and serve as a source of inspiration for new creative endeavors.

In my meandering armchair trek of the globe, I have gotten a glimpse into the character of many cultures by studying their folk art. I use the term folk art to mean primarily the creation of beautiful things used in daily life: the carpet on the floor, the tray for serving food, the stool to sit on, the bag to carry essential objects. In all cultures, the human family demonstrates a basic desire to create beauty in its personal environment. Beauty may mean different things to different cultures, but common to all is the need to bring creative expression into everyday activities.

In almost every culture that I have researched, the making and using of containers is significant to daily life. People everywhere use containers of some sort to organize, carry, and store things. And people everywhere make containers that are worthy of display. I have engineered my own daily appreciation of beauty—and the importance of a good container—through the collection of bags I present here. My intention is to provide knitters at all levels of expertise with a wide variety of construction and project choices. With that goal in mind, I have created a diverse group of bags that range in size, shape, color, use, and difficulty.

In size, the very smallest bag is what a friend calls the perfect credit card case: the Tajik coin purse that accompanies the Teahouse Sling Bag. The Korean Pocket Pouch is palm-sized, great for a personal gift, for others or yourself. On the large end of the spectrum, a small child could sit in the Floor Basket Shigra from Ecuador. Actually, I was able to sit in this bag myself before it was felted!

In color, I offer a panorama of hues that includes the natural off-white wool of the Irish Fish Creel and the neutral, but dramatic, combination of dark charcoal and pale sand in the bag from Congo. Dark, rich, intense colors predomi-

nate in my carpet-inspired bags from ancient Persia, Uzbekistan, and Turkey. Bright, vibrant colors characterize several bags from disparate places, from my Chinese Fish of Prosperity to my Zigzag Shigra from South America.

In shape, many of my bags are flat and rectangular. Some have interesting variations, such as the triangular edges of the Nigerian Yoruba Mask Bag or the fur stitch on the front of the Welsh Ysgrepan. Some bags are more three-dimensional—the cylindrical Tibetan Door Tassel Bag and the fully sculptural Bolivian Doll.

I trust that you, the reader, will invent a multitude of different uses for each bag! The decorative nature of some bags limits the kind and qualities of items they can carry. And always watch those pencils; you won't want them poking through the stitches of your beautiful finished bag and marking clothing! Some bags are designed to be functional, able to support weight and quantity. The small bags are perfect for carrying personal effects, and the large bags are ideal to stuff full of books, food, or . . . knitting!

Most of the bags will require an understanding of intermediate knitting skills, but be adventurous and don't be afraid to try new techniques. I have created a lot of unusual detail and incorporated many construction methods, including an I-cord knot and loop closure, a spiral wrapped edging, hem rolls, surface embroidery, origami folds, a cylinder knitted flat and finished in the round, and a bag made completely of I-cord that's held together with fringe.

Just as a splash of color or a visible brush stroke in a painting draws the eye, I have incorporated unique design elements in each bag to spark your interest. May each bag capture the attention of the knitter who makes it, the person who carries it, and the one who admires it. Perhaps *all* those people will be you. Enjoy!

The Maori, a tribe of Polynesian ancestry, were the first to land on the shores of New Zealand over one thousand years ago. In the past, the Maori were artisans of exquisite baskets and mats. Plaited baskets, or *kete*, were used daily in ancestral Maori life. Special kete were created for food preparation, production of hair oil, storage of clothing, babies' cradles, and almost any other situation that required a container. New Zealand's flax, called *harakeke*, was the most useful and versatile material to work with.

I was especially drawn to the pale golden warmth of the natural undyed fiber used in kete. Linen, spun from the stem fibers of flax, is my choice for these New Zealand bags; both the color and the texture capture the essential character of the Maori basketry. My spiral bag is intended to emulate the bottom of a coiled basket. Maori basket bags feature a wide variety of other intriguing design elements, including terraced flat panels, cylindrical shapes, and a variety of handle treatments. Fringe is my own unique design detail for the spiral bag.

I kept the drawstring bags more traditional in shape, and knitted them with a simple basketweave stitch so that they—surprise!—resemble woven baskets. While my nineteen-year-old daughter especially likes the small drawstring size, I definitely wanted to offer a larger size for people like me. My own "personal universe in a bag" must hold my knitting and my notions goody bag filled with tape measure, scissors, safety pins, a nail file, a small sketchbook, and just the right pencil. Then there are necessities like my wallet, my daytimer, a lipstick, a chopstick to secure my hair in a bun. . . . You get the idea. I only stop when my bag is full!

Spiral Bag

FINISHED SIZE 10" (25.5 cm) diameter, excluding fringe.

YARN Louet Euroflax Heather Chunky (100% wet-spun linen, 635 yd [581 m]/16 oz [454 g] cone). #72 camomile, 12 oz [341 g]/500 yd [458 m].

NEEDLES Size 7 [4.5 mm]: 2 double-pointed (dpn). Adjust needle size if necessary to obtain correct gauge.

NOTIONS Long straight sewing pins with colored heads; tapestry needle; size G/7 [4.5 mm] crochet hook for threading fringe strands.

GAUGE 3 sts in I-cord = ³⁄₈" (1 cm) in diameter, 5 rows = 1" (2.5 cm).

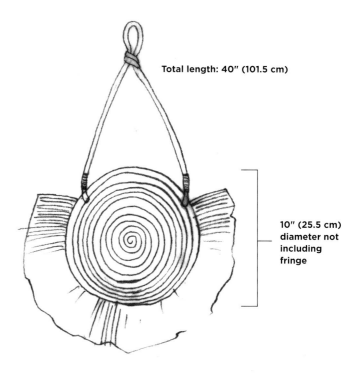

Total length: 40" (101.5 cm)

10" (25.5 cm) diameter not including fringe

SIDES OF BAG (make 2)
Leaving a 6" (15 cm) tail, CO 3 sts. Work in I-cord (see Techniques, page 142) for about 35 feet [10.67 m], or whatever I-cord length is needed to spiral around to make a 10" [25 cm] diameter disc. Work last row of I-cord as sl 1, k2tog, psso (see Abbreviations, page 146); cut yarn, leaving a 6" [15 cm] tail, and pull through remaining stitch to secure. With yarn tail threaded on tapestry needle, weave tail through center of I-cord. Weave in tail at CO end in same manner. Make second I-cord the same.

SEW SPIRAL TOGETHER Using one I-cord and working on a flat surface, take one end of the I-cord and

form a closed, flat circle. Then begin making a flat disc by spiraling the I-cord firmly around the center circle. Keep I-cord smooth and untwisted while you work. *When you've made 3 or 4 concentric circles, insert long straight pins with colored heads through the I-cord circles, working from the outer edges of the disc towards the center. The pins will help keep your spiral in place while you sew. Thread tapestry needle with about 18" (46 cm) of yarn (longer lengths might tangle, or shed fibers). Pick up piece in hand and working on the wrong side, insert threaded needle into the I-cord working from the outer edge of the circles toward the center, then insert the tapestry needle from the inner circles toward the outer edge*

Spiral Bag

(see Figure A). Thread needle with fresh yarn as needed. Remove pins after stitching each area.

NOTE When you're sewing through the new layers, overlap new stitches on one or two previously sewn layers to stabilize the sewn zigzag connections. Sew I-cord together compactly to avoid holes or open spaces between I-cord circles. Continue to pin and stitch around disc, repeating from * to * and securing new concentric layers together until disc diameter measures 10" (25.5 cm). Using second I-cord, make another disc to match first one. Steam block both discs. Let dry completely before finishing.

   With wrong sides facing, pin both discs together around the outer edges, leaving 10" (25.5 cm) unpinned for bag opening.

KNOTTED FRINGE The discs are attached to each other with the knotted fringe. Cut 3 strands, each 10" (25.5 cm) long, for each knot. With crochet hook, and beginning at one end of the unpinned edges, insert hook under 1 stitch from edge of each disc (see Figure B1). Working with 3 strands as one, pull half (5" [12.5 cm]) of the length through both edge sts and fold yarn at

edge; align all 3 strands side by side and even up yarn ends (see Figure B2). Tie an overhand knot, pull on strand ends and use tapestry needle inserted into knot center to force knot to tighten snugly against edge of disc/bag (see Figure B3). Repeat knotted fringe around the perimeter of bag to the other side of the bag top opening, fitting knots closely together.

STRAP Leaving 6" (15 cm) tail, CO 3 sts. Work in I-cord for about 45" (114.5 cm), or desired length. Complete last row of I-cord as sl 1, k2tog, psso. Cut yarn, leaving 6" (15 cm) tail, pull through last st, and tighten. Thread yarn tail on tapestry needle and weave through center of I-cord to secure. The yarn tail at CO edge is secured the same way. Using crochet hook, pull I-cord ends through both disc edges, one end at each side of the 10" (25.5 cm) top opening, then fold I-cord ends upwards 2" (5 cm) and tassel wrap (see Techniques, page 145) to secure strap to bag.

Easy option: Tie a square knot to secure strap ends. Steam block knots and fringe.

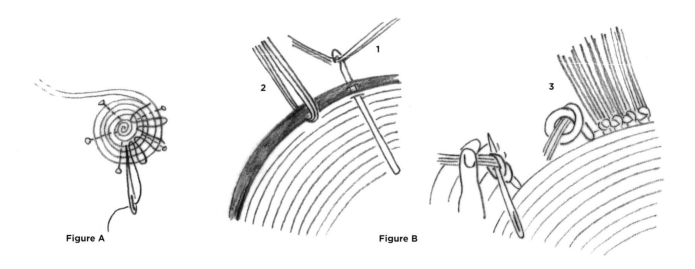

Figure A

Figure B

Basketweave
Drawstring

Basketweave
Drawstring

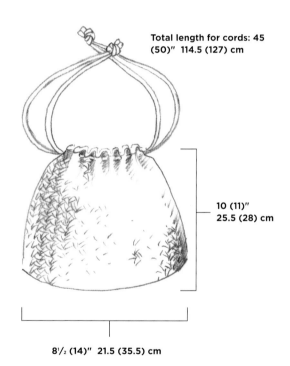

Total length for cords: 45 (50)" 114.5 (127) cm

10 (11)" 25.5 (28) cm

8¹⁄₂ (14)" 21.5 (35.5) cm

FINISHED SIZE 11″ (28 cm) deep × 14″ (35.5 cm) wide—large.

10″ (25.5 cm) deep × 8¹⁄₂″ (21.5 cm) wide—small.

YARN Louet Euroflax Heather Chunky (100% wetspun linen, 635 yd [581 m]/16 oz [454 g] cone). #72 camomile, 14 oz [397 g]/550 yd [503 m] for large bag.

8 oz [227 g]/320 yd [293 m] for small bag.

NEEDLES Size 10 [6 mm]—bag body. Size 7 [4.5 mm] set of 2 double-pointed (dpn)—I-cord. Adjust needle size if necessary to obtain correct gauge.

NOTIONS Tapestry needle.

GAUGE 18 sts and 16 rows = 4″ (10 cm) in basketweave stitch, using 2 strands of yarn held together throughout.

STITCH GUIDE
Basketweave stitch (multiple of 2 sts)
Row 1 (RS): K1, *pass right-hand needle behind first st

on left-hand needle and knit into the back of the second st, then knit into the front of the first st and slip both sts off needle*; rep from * to * across row, end k1.

Row 2: P2, *purl into the front of the second st, then purl into the front of the first st, slip sts off needle*; rep from * to * across row, end p2.

BODY, LARGE BAG Holding 2 strands of yarn together as one, CO 64 sts.

Foundation row: *P1, k1; rep from * to end of row. Repeat rows 1 and 2 of basketweave stitch until piece measures 22" (56 cm), ending RS facing.

BO row: Continue in basketweave pattern, working BO as follows: K1, knit into the back of second st, BO one st, knit into the front of first st, BO one st; cont in same manner across row.

NOTE The rem loop from the second st must be slipped off the needle *after* the front st is BO.

Fold work in half lengthwise, CO edge to BO edge and WS tog.

Both side seams: Cut 2 strands of yarn 18" (46 cm) long. Thread both strands on tapestry needle and weave side seams tog using invisible weaving (see Techniques, page 142). Weave in loose ends to WS of bag.

BODY, SMALL BAG Holding 2 strands of yarn tog, CO 40 sts. Work as for large bag until piece measures 20" (51 cm). Work BO row and finish same as large bag.

I-CORD STRAPS (make 2 for each bag)
Using 1 strand of yarn and dpn, CO 3 sts and work I-cord (see Techniques, page 142) for 50" (127 cm) for large bag, and 45" (114.5 cm) for small bag.

FINISHING Beginning at side edge, thread I-cord strap in and out of top edge of bag all the way around. Thread second cord the same way, starting at opposite side of bag. Tie knots in ends of I-cords and pull to draw closed.

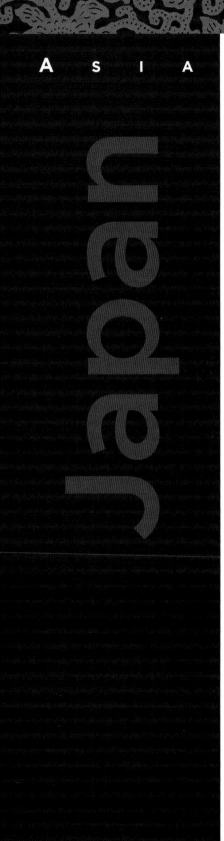
The ancient Chinese invented paper around the first century A.D. However, it was the medieval Japanese who integrated paper folding, or *origami*, into their culture. Today, origami has an appeal possibly broader than any other paper craft; it is a form of puzzle-solving, a branch of mathematics, a vocabulary for design. Put simply, origami is art, science, and play.

Origami is so distinctly Japanese that it seemed the perfect vehicle for creating a Japanese-style design, moving from folding paper to folding a knitted fabric. My bag does not specifically emulate a Japanese bag. In the past, the Japanese did not typically use bags; rather, they placed things in a large square of fabric and tied opposite corners together to carry the fabric like a sack. So I let origami inspire me to design two bags with a combination of elements derived from young girls' paper purses, wallets, and party containers. I defined the texture and color of the bags to be reminiscent of Japanese tastes.

For the small shoulder purse, I chose a natural main color of raw silk/tweedy cotton blend knitted in seed stitch with a black cotton I-cord edge; the colors remind me of bamboo thongs with black velvet straps. In the large tote bag, the deep blue echoes the peasant work kimono, which was often ikat-dyed with indigo. (See the Guatemalan section on page 128 for an explanation of ikat dyeing.) For this bag I've employed a twisted knit texture to emulate the woven reed mats used in Japanese homes. This stitch is compact and stable, yet not bulky, making it very suitable for maintaining the integrity of the knitted fabric and the shape of the folded bag with its many layers.

My set of illustrations are for the actual construction of the knitted bag. To keep the bags stable, the folds and seams are done a bit differently than they would be if the bags were constructed of paper, but the end result looks the same. You can enjoy them large or small.

Small
Origami
Bag

Small Origami Bag

FINISHED SIZE 6″ (15 cm) deep × 8″ (20.5 cm) wide.

YARN Webs Everett Silk (70% silk, 30% cotton, 1,120 yd [1,024 m]/16 oz [454 g] cone). #5610 beige (MC), 4 oz [114 g]/300 yd [275 m].

Brown Sheep Cotton Fleece (80% cotton, 20% wool, 215 yd [197 m]/100 g skein). #005 cavern (CC), 1 skein.

NEEDLES Size 3 [3.25 mm]—bag. Size 3 [3.25 mm] set of 2 double-pointed (dpn)—attached I-cord and strap. Adjust needle size if necessary to obtain correct gauge.

NOTIONS 2 buttons, 1″ (2.5 cm), or size of choice; long straight sewing pins with colored heads; a few inches of smooth waste yarn for invisible (provisional) CO.

GAUGE 18 sts and 28 rows = 4″ (10 cm) in seed stitch using Everett silk yarn.

STITCH GUIDE

Seed Stitch (even number of sts)
Row 1: *K1, p1; rep from * across row.
Row 2: *P1, k1; rep from * across row.
Repeat above 2 rows for patt.

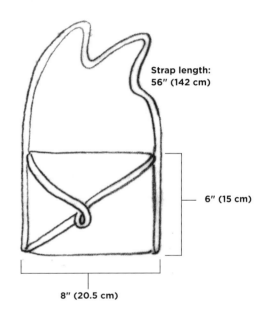

Strap length: 56″ (142 cm)

6″ (15 cm)

8″ (20.5 cm)

BAG SQUARE With MC cast on 64 sts. Work seed stitch until piece measures 14" (35.5 cm) from beg. BO in patt. Weave in loose ends to WS. Steam block square, let dry completely.

ATTACHED I-CORD BORDER (see Techniques, page 139). With WS of square facing, begin at 2" (5 cm) above right lower corner. With dpn, CC and waste yarn, CO 3 sts using invisible (provisional) CO (see Techniques, page 142). *Slide sts to other end of needle, k2, sl 1 as if to knit. Insert right needle into the edge of square and pick up a stitch, pass the slipped st over the newly made stitch*. Rep from * to * up to the first corner.

AT FIRST CORNER, [work 3" (7.5 cm) of unattached I-cord (see Techniques, page 142). Loop the 3" (7.5 cm) of I-cord clockwise back upon itself to create a button-hole loop, then work attached I-cord again to next corner. At this corner, work 3 rows of unattached I-cord to create adequate fullness to cover 90-degree turn, then resume working attached I-cord to next corner.] Repeat all instructions within brackets around 4 sides of square, finishing I-cord by removing waste yarn at CO edge and grafting beg sts to those in final I-cord row (see Techniques, page 143). Using CC threaded on tapestry needle, whipstitch (see Techniques, page 145) button loops to secure twist. Steam block entire piece again, let dry completely.

STRAP Using dpn and CC, CO 3 sts. Work I-cord for 56" (142 cm) unstretched. Work last I-cord row as sl 1, k 2tog, psso (see Abbreviations, page 146). Weave in loose ends.

FINISHING (see Figures). Place bag RS up with loop corners at top and bottom (Figure A). Fold bottom up and match loop corners (Figure B). Mark folded edge in thirds and pin two seams perpendicular to folded edge, at ⅓ and ⅔ marks (Figure B). With MC threaded on tapestry needle, backstitch (see Techniques, page 139) from folded edge up to, but not including, I-cord (Figure B). Fold left corner back upon bag by opening and turning inside out, WS together. Fold right corner back, overlapping left corner (Figure C). Pin and sew left/right/overlapping corners, working from WS (inside of bag). Fold loop corner flaps down and mark for button placement (Figure D). Pin I-cord strap centered over side seams (Figure E). Using MC, whipstitch onto bag working from WS. Sew on buttons. Weave in all loose ends to WS. Lightly steam seams to set.

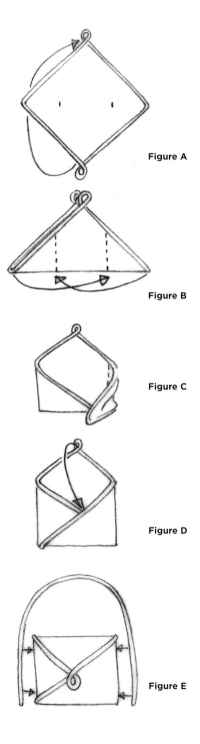

Figure A

Figure B

Figure C

Figure D

Figure E

Large Origami Bag

FINISHED SIZE 16½" (42 cm) deep × 18" (46 cm) wide.

YARN Plymouth Blu Jeans (100% indigo dyed cotton, 118 yd [108 m]/50 g). #04 dark indigo (MC), 13 skeins.

Plymouth Blu Jeans (100% natural cotton, 118 yd [108 m]/50 g). #01 white (CC), 2 skeins.

NEEDLES Size 3 [3.25 mm]—bag. Size 3 [3.25 mm] set of 2 double-pointed (dpn)—attached I-cord and strap. Adjust needle size if necessary to obtain correct gauge.

NOTIONS 2 buttons, 2" (5 cm), or size of choice; long straight sewing pins with colored heads; few inches of smooth waste yarn for invisible (provisional) CO.

GAUGE 22 sts and 34 rows = 4" (10 cm) in pattern stitch.

STITCH GUIDE

Twisted knit basketweave stitch
Row 1 (RS): *K1 through the back loop (tbl); rep from * across row.
Row 2: Purl.

BAG SQUARE With MC yarn, CO 216 sts. Work twisted knit basketweave stitch until piece measures 38" (96.5 cm) from beg. BO in patt. Steam block square, let dry completely.

ATTACHED I-CORD BORDER (see Techniques, page 139). Using dpn, waste yarn and CC, follow instructions as for small bag.

DOUBLE I-CORD STRAP Using dpn and CC yarn, CO 7 sts, turn work. *K4, yarn forward, slip 3 sts as if to purl, turn. Rep from * until strap is 67" (170 cm) long. BO as follows: K2tog, k1, BO 1 st, k1, BO 1 st, p1, BO 1 st, p2tog, BO. Cut yarn and thread through last st to secure. Work finishing as for small origami bag.

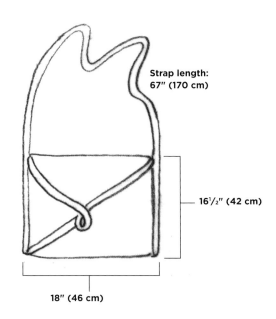

Strap length: 67" (170 cm)

16½" (42 cm)

18" (46 cm)

China

Throughout history, much of China's craft activity has been centered around the numerous festivals corresponding to the ancient lunar calendar. Local artisans displayed and sold a variety of craftwork, including textile arts. Embroidery skills were showcased on brightly colored shoulder bags or waist purses.

Perhaps the most original examples of folk embroidery are the symbols found on children's clothing and handmade toys. The likeness of a dog or pig encouraged evil spirits to pass over the child, because it wouldn't be worth the spirits' time to disturb a common animal. Elaborately sewn tiger shoes with an additional set of embroidered eyes ensured that young children would see more clearly where they were walking. Fish symbolized surplus and abundance. A fish mobile hanging over a baby's crib would express hope for a plentiful life.

I wanted to capture the whimsical expression found in children's articles and I deemed the symbol for abundance most appropriate for a purse! The shape of my Fish of Prosperity is similar to a small cotton fabric bag I saw in a folk art collection. Chinese red is so distinctively a warm, intense hue that I chose it for the main body. I wanted the stability of a felted bag, so I used wool for the fish, but the embroidery is all cotton, which is the material most used for bags in China. The sheen of the cotton emulates silk, sometimes used as embroidery fiber.

Expanding on the Chinese symbol for abundance, the Fish Lips bag is an expression of my own childhood. I remember drawing pictures of fish with these funny lips, and then smacking my own lips in the way I drew them. I thought I was quite the entertainer at the ripe old age of seven. The hand-painted yarn I chose for this bag felts to a wonderful texture and gives the colors an "underwater" look.

Fish *of* Prosperity

Fish *of* Prosperity

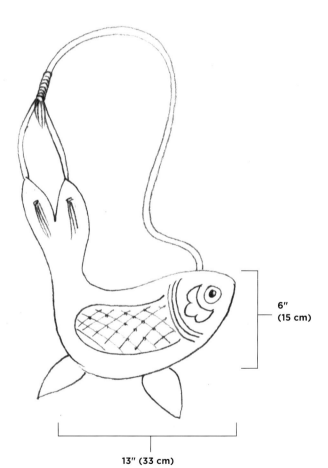

6"
(15 cm)

13" (33 cm)

FINISHED SIZE Fish body, 6" (15 cm) deep × 13" (33 cm) wide.

YARN Classic Elite Montera (50% llama/50% wool, 127 yd [116 m]/100 g). #3858 cintachi red, 2 skeins.

Classic Elite Provence (100% mercerized Egyptian cotton, 256 yd [234 m]/125 g). #2657 DeNimes blue, #2694 China trade jade, #2633 sun dried yellow, #2619 zinnia flower, small amounts of each color for embroidery.

NEEDLES Size 10 (6 mm). Adjust needle size if necessary to obtain the correct gauge.

NOTIONS 2 mother-of-pearl buttons, 1" (2.5 cm); 2 shiny black beads, 1/4" (6 mm); stitch holder; tapestry needle; long straight sewing pins with colored heads.

GAUGE 12 sts and 16 rows = 4" (10 cm) in stockinette stitch (before felting).

FISH BODY (work in St st throughout) CO 12 sts and purl 1 row.

NOTE Use Cable CO (see Techniques, page 140) at the beg of next 8 rows, working as follows: CO 4 sts, knit to end of row. CO 4 sts, purl to end of row. CO 6 sts, knit to end. CO 2 sts, purl to end. CO 4 sts, knit to end. CO 2 sts, purl to end. CO 2 sts, knit to end. CO 2 sts, purl to end—(38 sts).

Increase rows: [Inc 1 st, knit to row end.
Next row: Inc 1 st, purl to row end.
Next row: Inc 1 st, knit to end.
Next row: Purl.] Work between [ ] 5 times—(53 sts). Work next 6 rows as follows: Knit 1 row. Inc 1 st, purl to end of row. Knit 1 row. Purl 1 row. Inc 1 st, knit to end. Purl 1 row—(55 sts at nose point). Work next 4 rows as follows: BO 2 sts, knit to end. Purl 1 row. BO 2 sts, knit to end. P17, place these sts on holder, BO 9, purl to end—(25 sts rem on needle,17 sts on holder for tail). Finish nose: BO 3 sts at beg of next 4 rows—(13 sts).
Next row: Bind off rem sts. Weave in loose ends to WS of work.

TAIL Place 17 sts from holder onto needle and with RS facing attach yarn at right.
[K2tog, knit to end. Purl 1 row.] Work 5 times—(12 sts). Work 10 rows even.
Next row: (RS) Inc 1 st each end of row—(14 sts). Work 3 rows even. [Inc 1 st each end of knit row. Purl 1 row] 3 times—(20 sts). [Inc 1 st, knit to end. Purl 1 row. Inc 1 st each end of knit row. Purl 1 row.] 2 times—(26 sts).
NOTE Tailfins are not symmetrical; follow separate instructions for each.

First tailfin: K13, place rem 13 sts on holder. Work as follows: P2tog, p to end. Inc 1 st, knit to end. Purl 1 row. Knit 1 row. P2tog, purl to end. K2tog, knit to end. P2tog, purl to end. Knit 1 row. P2tog, purl to end. [K2tog, knit to end.

P2tog, purl to end] 3 times—(3 sts rem). Sl 1, k2tog, psso (see Abbreviations, page 146). Cut yarn and thread through rem st, pull to secure. Weave in loose ends.

Second tailfin: Remove 13 sts from holder and place sts onto needle. With RS facing, attach yarn and k13 sts. Work as follows: Purl 1 row. K2tog, knit to row end. Purl 1 row. Knit 1 row. Purl 1 row. K2tog, knit to end. Purl 1 row. Knit 1 row. P2tog, purl to end. [K2tog, knit to end. Purl 1 row. K2tog, knit to end. P2tog, purl to end] 2 times—(4 sts). K2tog, knit to end. Purl 1 row. Sl 1, k2tog, psso. Finish off same as first tailfin.

TO MAKE SECOND SIDE OF FISH Read instructions as reverse stockinette; i.e., purl where it says to knit, and knit where it says to purl. This is the easiest way to reverse all shaping.

LOWER FORWARD FIN Work in garter st. CO 9 sts. Knit 2 rows.

NOTE Garter st short row wraps remain in place, do not hide.

Short row: (see Techniques, page 144) K4, wrap and turn, knit to end.
Next row: Knit, inc 1 st each end of row—(11 sts). Knit 5 rows.
Next row: SSK, knit to end. Knit 2 rows. [SSK, knit to last 2 sts, k2tog. Knit 3 rows] 2 times—(6 sts).
Next row: SSK, k2tog twice—(3 sts).
Next row: Sl 1, k2tog, psso.

LOWER REAR FIN Work in garter st. CO 8 sts. Knit 2 rows.
Short row: K4, wrap and turn, knit to end. Knit 4 rows. [Knit across row to last 2 sts, k2tog. Knit 3 rows] 2 times—(6 sts).

Next row: SSK, k2, k2tog—(4 sts). Knit 2 rows.
Next row: K2, k2tog—(3 sts). Knit 1 row. Sl 1, k2tog, psso.
Cut yarn and pull through rem st to secure. Weave in loose ends.

STRAPS Cut 3 strands yarn 100" (254 cm) long. At edge of opening near head, insert strands to halfway (50") [127 cm]. Twist strands to make a twisted cord (see Techniques, page 145), tie knot at end to secure. Finished cord length 47" (119.5 cm) when tied. Cut 6 strands 35" (89 cm) long. Insert 3 strands through top of each tailfin to halfway (17") [43 cm]. Twist strands into cord, tie knot at end to secure.

ASSEMBLE With purl sides tog, pin all the way around. Whipstitch (see Techniques, page 145) layers tog evenly, leaving top of fish open from middle of bound off sts on curved head 9" (23 cm) toward back of fish. Whipstitch lower fins in place.

FELTING (See Techniques, page 141). After felting, pull fish into shape if necessary, then flatten and smooth by pressing firmly with flat of hand. Let dry completely.

FINISHING Embroider (see Techniques, page 141 for embroidery stitches used on this bag) with cotton yarn on both sides of bag using outline or stem stitch for shapes, and overlay/couching for "scales." Follow colors as shown in photo. For each fringe tassel on tailfin, cut 3 pieces 6" (15 cm) long. Pull folded strands through tail-fins as shown (Figure A), and pull cut ends through loop (Figure A). Pull strands snugly to secure. Sew on button for eye with bead over button center. Overlap 2 tailfin straps with head strap for 3" (7.5 cm); tassel wrap (see Techniques, page 145) with orange cotton for 1½" (3.8 cm). Weave in loose ends to WS of work.

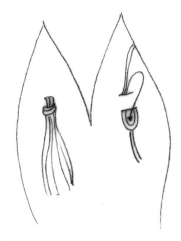

Figure A

Fish Lips Purse

Fish Lips Purse

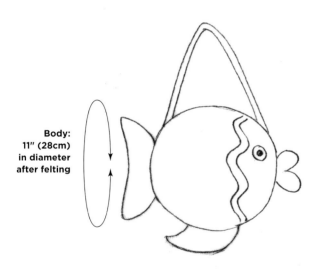

Body: 11" (28cm) in diameter after felting

FINISHED SIZE Fish body is about 16" (40.5 cm) before felting; 11" (28 cm) in diameter after felting.

YARN Brown Sheep Handpaint Originals (70% mohair, 30% wool, 88 yd [81 m]/50 g). HP 100 majesty (MC), 6 skeins. HP05 black cherry (CC), 1 skein.

NEEDLES Size 11 (8 mm)—fish body. Size 10½ (6.5 mm) set of 2 double-pointed (dpn)—lips. Adjust needle size to obtain the correct gauge.

NOTIONS 2 shank-type buttons 1½" (3.8 cm) for eyes; tapestry needle, long straight sewing pin with colored head to mark center of I-cord.

GAUGE 11 sts and 14 rows = 4" (10 cm) in stockinette stitch, before felting.

NOTE Work 2 strands of yarn held together as one throughout. Before knitting, wind CC into 2 balls same size.

BAG BODY With 2 strands of MC held tog, CO 16 sts. Working in St st throughout, follow intarsia (see Techniques, page 142) chart beg with the foundation row, then work rows 1–54. BO on row 55. Use knitted CO (see Techniques, page 143) to add more than 1 st in a row; use k1f&b (see Abbreviations, page 146) inc to add 1 st. To work second side of bag, reverse chart by working odd-numbered rows as WS, and even numbers as RS. Place WS of bag together and whipstitch (see Techniques, page 145) around, leaving 11" (28 cm) unstitched for top opening.

I-CORD LIPS With MC and dpn, CO 4 sts and work I-cord (see Techniques, page 142) for 12" (30.5 cm). Work last row as k2tog twice, BO. Cut yarn and thread through last st to secure. Mark center (6") [15 cm] of I-cord with straight pin. Attach end of I-cord onto edge of bag (see photo for placement), place center of cord right next to end. Using 2 strands of MC threaded on tapestry needle, whipstitch over cord and to edge of bag. Attach other end of cord same way, right next to the center.

LOWER FIN With MC and larger needles, pick up 20 sts along lower edge of bag, centered on body curve. Knit 1 row. Working in garter stitch, [dec 1 st at beg of row and inc 1 st at the end of same row. Knit 1 row.] 5 times—(20 sts, 10 rows).
Next row: BO 2 sts, knit to end.
Next row: Cable CO (see Techniques, page 140) 2 sts, knit to row end. BO all sts.

TAILFIN With MC and larger needles, pick up 20 sts along bag body curve for tail. Knit 1 row. Working in garter st, [inc 1 st each end of every 4th row] 3 times—(26 sts, 12 rows).

Work short row (see Techniques, page 144) as follows: [K7 sts, wrap and turn, knit to end.
Next row: K4, wrap and turn, knit to end.] Knit 1 row. Repeat between [ ] once. Short row wraps remain in place, do not hide. BO.

STRAP: Cut 4 strands MC and 2 strands CC each 80" (203.5 cm) long. Insert all 6 strands to halfway (40") [101.5 cm] into bag at edge of top opening. Braid with 3 sections, each containing 4 strands. Attach end of braid to other edge of top opening by threading braid ends into tapestry needle and inserting into bag from RS to WS; tie knot and weave in ends on WS.

FELTING (See Techniques, page 141.) Felt bag twice, running it through hot wash cycles for additional body. Pull bag into shape if necessary, then hand press flat with palm of hand. Let dry completely.

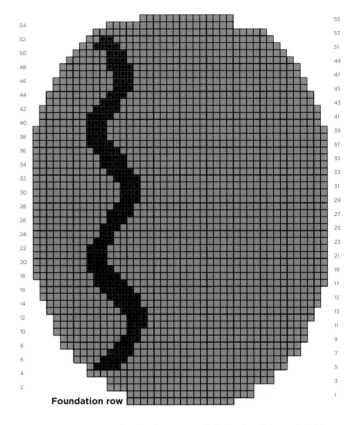

■ (MC) HP 100 majesty

✦ (CC) HP 05 black cherry

Work chart in St st, using 2 strands of MC held together as one for MC sts, and 2 strands of CC held together as one for CC sts.

First side of bag: Purl foundation row on WS. Begin with row 1 (RS), knit odd-numbered rows reading chart from right to left, and purl even-numbered rows reading chart from left to right. BO on row 55.

Second side of bag: To reverse chart, knit foundation row, then purl odd-numbered rows and knit even-numbered rows. BO on row 55.

A Korean woman's traditional garment, called a *hanbok*, is characterized by the simple lines of a short bolero-like jacket and a wrap skirt with no pockets. Western-style dress is now pervasive in Korea, but hanbok are still worn on ceremonial occasions, at special social events with a Korean theme, and on traditional holidays. Because hanbok have no pockets, a woman carried a purse, or *jumeoni*, suspended by a drawstring from her bodice or within her skirts, which were layered over billowing pants. There were two basic designs for the jumeoni: a round pouch gathered into irregular folds at the top; and a somewhat triangular one pleated into set folds and closed by a drawstring. Historically, nine folds indicated that the bag belonged to a person of court status; such a bag would most likely be red or another bright color of silk. Commoners' bags would have only three folds, and would be made of hemp or cotton in white, pale pink, green, or gray. Bags had numerous functions and could contain items such as a spoon, chopsticks, a fan, medicine, and incense; as well as soybeans, which were used as a sort of good luck charm.

The pleated, triangular shape of the jumeoni intrigued me. I combined elements of the pouches belonging to the two social strata, using a clear pale color, a simple drawstring arrangement, and adding surface embroidery reminiscent of a silk brocade fabric. The small size is perfect for holding jewelry when I travel.

Folds *of* Function
Pocket Pouch

Folds *of* Function
Pocket Pouch

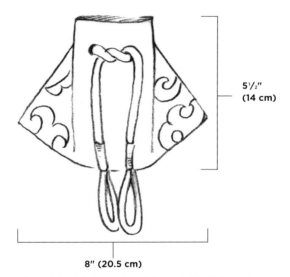

5¹/₂″ (14 cm)

8″ (20.5 cm)

FINISHED SIZE 8″ (20.5 cm) wide × 5¹/₂″ (14 cm) deep, unfolded.

YARN Patons Grace (100% mercerized cotton, 136 yd [125m]/50 g). #60603 pale apricot (MC), #60604 melon (CC). 1 ball each color.

NEEDLES Size 2 (2.75 mm)—bag. Size 2 (2.75 mm) set of 2 double-pointed (dpn)—I-cord. Adjust needle size if necessary to obtain the correct gauge.

NOTIONS Size C/2 (3 mm) crochet hook; tapestry needle; water-erasable marking pen (available at fabric store); stitch markers.

GAUGE 26 sts and 36 rows = 4″ (10 cm) in stockinette stitch.

STITCH GUIDE

Make 1 (m1): On knit side of work, insert left needle tip from front to back under the running thread between both needle tips, then knit lifted thread through the back strand to twist and close. On purl side, insert left needle tip from back to front under the running thread, purl st as usual (see Techniques, page 143 for illustrations).

NOTE Slip markers from left needle to right needle on every row.

With MC, CO 46 sts, purl 1 row.
Row 1: K1, m1, k12, place marker (pm), slip 1 st purlwise, k18, pm, slip 1 purlwise, k12, m1, k1—48 sts.
Row 2: P1, m1, purl to last st, m1, p1—50 sts.
Cont increases in same manner every row for 3 rows, slipping st purlwise after markers on knit rows—56 sts. Work even in St st until work measures 1″ (2.5 cm) from CO; work buttonhole row 1 as follows: K12, yo, k2tog, k4, sl 1, k5, yo, k2tog, k5, yo, k2tog, k4, sl 1, k5, yo, K2tog, knit to end—56 sts. Continue St st with slipped sts for 3 rows. When work measures 1⅛″ (3.5 cm) from CO, work buttonhole row 2 as follows: K5, yo, k2tog, k11, sl 1, k18, sl 1, k12, yo, k2tog, k4—56 sts. Continue St st and slipped sts as established until piece measures 5½″ (14 cm), ending with WS side facing. Knit one row on WS of work for turning ridge. On RS, continue St st and slipped sts until work measures 4″ (10 cm) above

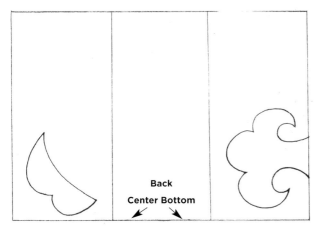

Back
Center Bottom

Figure A

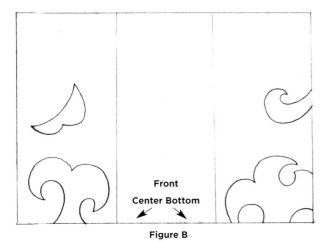

Front
Center Bottom

Figure B

I-CORD DRAWSTRING With CC and dpn, CO 3 sts. Knit I-cord (see Techniques, page 142) for 24" (61 cm), working last row as sl 1, k2tog, psso (see Abbreviations, page 146).
Cut yarn and thread through rem st to secure.

FINISHING Draw designs (see Techniques, page 141) onto bag with water-erasable marking pen (see embroidery Figures A and B). With CC yarn threaded on tapestry needle, embroider designs using stem stitch (see Techniques, page 141). Fold bag in half at turning ridge, and with MC yarn threaded on tapestry needle, weave side seams together using invisible weaving for St st. Single crochet (see Techniques, page 144) around top edge of bag with MC. Beginning at a center front buttonhole, insert I-cord drawstring in and out of each buttonhole around the bag and return to the front (see Figure C).

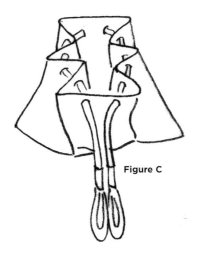

Figure C

garter st turning ridge. Repeat buttonhole row 2. Work even in est patt for 3 rows. Repeat buttonhole row 1. Work 3 rows even.

Decrease row 1: K1, ssk, work even in est patt to last 3 sts, k2tog, k1.

Decrease row 2: P1, p2tog, purl to last 3 sts, ssp (see Abbreviations, page 146), p1. Cont dec 1 st at each end of row for 3 rows—46 sts. Purl 1 row. Remove markers and BO. Weave in loose ends to WS of work.

I-cord loops: Fold 3" (7.5 cm) of I-cord back on itself at each end to form loops, and tassel wrap (see Techniques, page 145) with MC for 1" (2.5 cm) to secure. Weave in loose ends to WS of work.

Nepal

The famous city of Kathmandu, founded A.D. 700, is the capital of the independent kingdom of Nepal, which is situated between India and Tibet. A landlocked country, Nepal has always had a many-textured internal life, serving as a home to over thirty-six ethnic groups and over fifty languages.

The religion of Nepal is a mixture of Buddhism and Hinduism, and the monks who traveled southwest China, Nepal, and Tibet traditionally carried large bags. Some were brightly colored, some were faded by time—but beautifully toned, nonetheless. The monks carried all their earthly goods in these bags, so pockets inside and out were a useful feature. Since I love the organization that pockets provide, I designed this bag with five separate spaces in addition to the spacious capacity of the main compartment. Now, if I could just remember which pocket has my keys. . . .

Monk's
Travel
Satchel

Monk's Travel Satchel

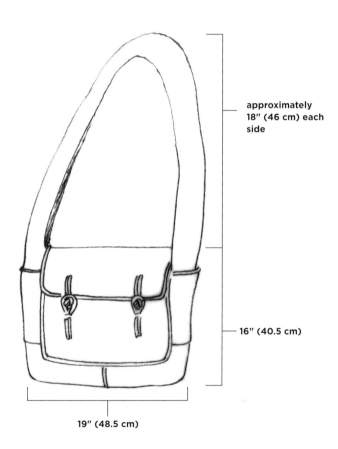

approximately 18" (46 cm) each side

16" (40.5 cm)

19" (48.5 cm)

FINISHED SIZE 16" (40.5 cm) deep × 19" (48.5 cm) wide.

YARN Brown Sheep Cotton Fleece (80% cotton, 20% wool, 215 yd [197 m]/100 g). #005 cavern (color A), 3 skeins. #880 twilight green (color B), 2 skeins. #930 candy apple (color C), 2 skeins.

NEEDLE Size 4 (3.5 mm) circular (circ)—2 pair each 29" (73.5 cm) long (for border of the back of the bag). Size 4 (3.5 mm) set of 2 double-pointed (dpn)—I-cord. Size 5 (3.75) or larger—for binding off. Adjust needle size if necessary to obtain the correct gauge.

NOTIONS Size E/4 (3.5 mm) crochet hook; tapestry needle; long straight sewing pins with colored heads.

GAUGE 22 sts and 34 rows = 4" (10 cm) in St st. 22 sts and 36 rows = 4" (10 cm) in seed st.

STITCH GUIDE

Seed stitch (2 st rep; + 1)
All rows: *K1, pl; rep from * to last st, k1.

GUSSET/STRAP With A and circ needle, CO 33 sts. Work in seed st for 74" (188 cm). Change to C and knit 2 rows. BO (1 garter ridge).

GUSSET POCKETS (make 2) With A, CO 33 sts, work in seed st 7½" (19 cm). Change to C, knit 1 row. BO on WS of work.

FRONT With B, CO 77 sts. Work St st for 12" (30.5 cm). Change to seed st for 2" (5 cm)—front measures 14" (35.5 cm) from CO edge. Bind off.

BACK AND FLAP With B, CO 77 sts. Work St st until back measures 14" (35.5 cm). Change to seed st and work 7" (18 cm) more for front flap. BO in patt.

BACK POCKET With B, cast on 55 sts. Work seed st for 8" (20.5 cm). BO in patt. Finished pocket measures 8" (20.5 cm) long × 10" (25.5 cm) wide.

INSIDE POCKET With C, CO 45 sts. Work in seed st for 4" (10 cm). Bind off in pattern. Finished pocket measures 4" (10 cm) long × 8" (20.5 cm) wide.

FINISHING

Front bag: With RS facing, using C and circ needle, beg at upper right corner, pick up 1 st in each BO st across the seed st top; pick up 2 sts every 3 rows along selvedge edge; pick up st for st across bottom edge; and 2 sts for every 3 rows along second selvedge edge. Turn work and knit to end. Turn work and BO using a needle 1 or 2 sizes larger than size used to work front. Cut yarn leaving 6" (15 cm) tail, insert through last loop to secure. Using C yarn tail threaded on tapestry needle, join edging beg and end together using a short 1 row seam in backstitch (see Techniques, page 139).

Back bag RS facing: Along selvedge edge measure 6"

(15 cm) from seed stitch BO. Begin here and pick up sts all around bag, using 1 circ needle to pick up and second circ needle to knit, working border in one piece. Pick up 2 sts for every 3 rows along selvedge edges, and st for st along CO and BO edges. Turn work, knit 1 row. BO and finish as for bag front. Weave in all ends and steam block all pieces. Lightly press St st surface. Lay flat to dry completely.

Assemble:

1. With A, backstitch center bottom edge of seed stitch gusset/strap.

2. Use straight pins as markers. Place first markers 7" (18 cm) from center bottom both ways on both edges of gusset. Mark 14" (35.5 cm) from first marker both ways, both edges (see Figure A).

3. Place gusset pockets with top edge 2" (5 cm) down (toward center back) from second marker. Pin in place. With A, backstitch lower edge of each gusset pocket in place (see Figure B). Remove all pins.

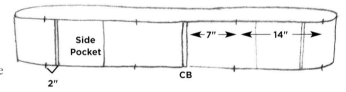

Figure A

Figure B

4. With RS tog, pin front of bag to gusset, matching lower corners to first markers, and top of bag to second markers. Using C, and slip-stitch crochet (see Techniques, page 145) seam pieces together. Remove pins.

NOTE Red edging is not in the seam.

5. Place interior 4" (10 cm) × 8" (20.5 cm) seed st pocket on WS of back, with lower edge of pocket about 4½" (11.5 cm) above bottom edge of bag, and centered side to side. Pin in place. With C, backstitch around sides and bottom of pocket; backstitch vertical seam down center of pocket to create 2 pocket spaces.

6. Place back 8" (20.5 cm) × 10" (25.5 cm) pocket on RS of back of bag, with lower edge about 1½" (3.8 cm) above bottom edge of bag, and centered side to side. Pin in place. Using B, backstitch around sides and bottom of pocket.

7. Mark 14" (35.5 cm) from lower edge on back/flap piece. With RS of gusset and back together, match up 14" (35.5 cm) markers and lower corners at 7" (18 cm) markers. Pin in place. With B, join pieces together using slip stitch crochet seam.

NOTE Red edging is not in the seam.

I-CORD CLOSURES (make four I-cords, two of each length) With dpn, work I-cord (see Techniques, page 142) until 10" (25.5 cm) long—for knots. Work second set of I-cords until 6" (15 cm) long—for loops. Fold 10" (25.5 cm) I-cord in half, tie overhand knot in folded end; place on bag flap 3" (7.5 cm) from side edge. Whipstitch (see Techniques, page 145) onto bag from WS, catching just the back side of I-cord sts. On RS of work, whipstitch over the end of I-cord, close to the knot. With pins, mark closure loop pieces for placement on front of bag and whipstitch onto bag from wrong side, catching just the back side of I-cord sts. On RS of work, whipstitch over end and 1½" (3.8 cm) up from end to form button loop. Remove all pins, weave in all ends to WS.

Tibet

Tibet is called The Roof of the World, an apt description for a country with an average altitude in excess of 12,000 feet (3,650 meters). Until the Chinese invasion in 1949, in the days when Tibet was an independent country, monks constituted as much as twenty percent of the male population. A monk's typical garb was a deep red, ankle-length woolen garment and a hat of the color associated with his particular sect.

Before the Chinese takeover, monasteries were centers for education, art, and public worship. Although many monasteries were closed or destroyed during the 1960s, today some of them are being restored. Typically, a monastery's brightly painted doors were embellished with large woven tubular tassels on either side. These ornaments were richly colored and ornately embellished, and might have fringe at the top and bottom. After seeing pictures of Tibetan monasteries and their wonderfully decorated doors, I knew that I had to have my very own giant tassel! So I designed this tubular bag, which is felted to a supple texture to maintain its cylindrical shape. Tibetan monastery door tassels were often decorated with floral or cloud motifs, or other designs inspired by nature. My own inspiration from nature is a simplified wave motif repeated in aubergine on a red background, reminiscent of the red of the monks' robes. The splash of blazing orange is my surprise treat for the knitter and the bag wearer.

Monastery Door
Tassel Bag

FINISHED SIZE 12″ (30.5 cm) deep × 6″ (15 cm) in diameter.

YARN Baabajoe's Wool Pak (pure New Zealand wool, 14 ply/310 yd [284 m]/250 g hank). #06 red (MC), #15 blaze (A), #35 aubergine (B), 1 hank of each color.

NEEDLES Size 9 (5.5mm) circular (circ) 24″ (61 cm) length—bag body. Size 9 (5.5 mm) set of 4 or 5 double-pointed (dpn)—bag base. Size 4 (3.5 mm) circ 24″ (61 cm) length—seam rolls.

NOTE This last needle size is approximate; the size should be small enough to pick up loops from the back side without pulling the stitch. Adjust needle size if necessary to obtain the correct gauge.

NOTIONS 2 clothespins; tapestry needle; stitch marker.

GAUGE 13½ sts and 17 rows = 4″ (10 cm) in stockinette stitch, before felting.

NOTE Bag is knitted from the top down. The tube is knitted flat, then joined at the bottom to finish in the round. Seam is whipstitched unobtrusively and is virtually invisible after felting.

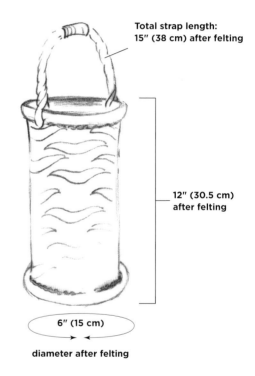

Total strap length: 15″ (38 cm) after felting

12″ (30.5 cm) after felting

6″ (15 cm)

diameter after felting

BAG BODY With MC and larger circ needle, CO 84 sts. Purl 1 row. Work 4 rows St st. Change to A and seam for top roll as follows: With smaller circ needle, pick up all 84 loops of CO edge. Fold work with WS together, and with needles parallel, *knit together first st from each needle. (It works best to knit into the back of the loops picked up.) Rep from * to end of row. Knit 1 row—1 garter ridge in color A. Change to MC, knit 1 row, purl 1 row.

Buttonhole row: K20, yo, k2tog, k40, yo, k2tog, k20—(84 sts). Purl 1 row.

Begin chart with row 1, working in combination of intarsia and Fair Isle techniques (see Techniques, pages 141 and 142). (For each wave motif use a 6½ yd (6 m) strand of yarn; strand the MC background as necessary to accomplish intarsia.) Work chart 3 times—72 rows complete.

Change to A, knit 2 rows. Change to MC, knit 8 rows St st.

Seam for roll: With smaller circ needle, pick up all purl loops in A closest to needle (9 rows back). Fold last 8 rows with WS together and with needles parallel, *knit together first st from each needle. Rep from * to end of row. Change to A, join work into circ, placing marker to indicate beginning of rnd, work next 22 rnds as follows, changing to dpn as necessary.

Rnd 1: Knit.
Rnd 2: Purl.
Rnd 3: [K12, k2tog] 6 times—(78 sts).
Rnd 4 and all even numbered rounds: Knit.
Rnd 5: [K11, k2tog] 6 times—(72 sts).
Rnd 7: [K10, k2tog] 6 times—(66 sts).

Continue in this manner dec 6 sts every other rnd until [k 5, k2tog] 6 times is complete, ending with the dec rnd—(36 sts). Continue dec in same manner on *every rnd* until k2tog around is complete—6 sts rem. Remove marker, cut yarn and draw end through all loops to secure. Weave ends in on WS. Whipstitch (see Techniques, page 145) tube seam using MC on background and B on motif colors.

TWISTED CORD HANDLE With A cut 6 strands 80" (203 cm) long. Twist all strands together as one until diameter is about ¼" (6 mm). Test the cord and allow it to twist back on itself until the diameter is ½" (1.3 cm), but do not secure the twist yet. With a straight pin, mark the midway point from either end. Insert one end of twisted strands through buttonhole in bag from WS until end extends past the midway mark by 1½" (3.8 cm) (see Figure A). Pinch the ends and the midway mark together with clothespin, remove straight pin. Let bag hang and allow cord to twist. Leave clothespin in place to hold twist until finishing.

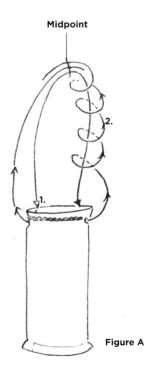

Midpoint

Figure A

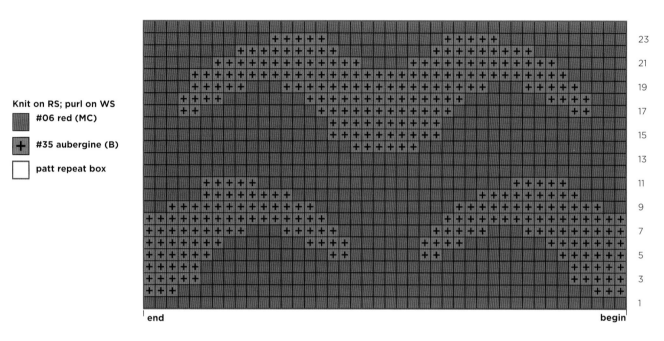

Knit on RS; purl on WS

■ #06 red (MC)

+ #35 aubergine (B)

□ patt repeat box

end   begin

Work 42 chart sts 2 times—84 sts. Work 24 chart rows 3 times—72 rows. Return to text instructions after completing chart.

Insert other end of twisted strands into remaining buttonhole from WS until end placement overlaps midway by 1½" (3.8 cm). This step will require you to wrap the cord (rather than letting it hang and twist itself) until its twist matches the first.

Cut ends should overlap 3" (7.5 cm) at midpoint of handle. Cut 2 strands MC 20" (51 cm) long. Using both strands together as one, tassel wrap (see Techniques,

page 145) the overlapping ends of handle to finish and secure.

FELTING (see Techniques, page 141). Felt bag twice for extra body. With palm of hand press bottom flat, pull sides of tube to shape, if necessary. Fill bag with rolled towels to keep cylinder upright. Let dry completely.

The craft of pile weaving either originated or was perfected in ancient Persia. Both the forms and the color palette used in these marvelous complex designs are nothing short of amazing, since only the most primitive tools were available to the nomadic cultures. Portability was essential, so looms were often little more than two parallel poles embedded in the ground. The beams may have been greased with clay to hold the warp threads stretched across them in a definite order. A knife, a pair of scissors, a comb to beat down the weft, a cord to protect the weft from damage, and warp wideners rounded out the small cache of tools used in this craft.

One of the oldest cultivated plants of the Far and Middle East, cotton has been used in Persia since early times for the foundation warp and weft of carpets. The pile, or knotted surface design, is usually sheep's wool or camel hair. Almost all carpets are knotted with either the Turkish (Gordes) or the Persian (Senneh) knot. Neither are knots in the normal sense of the word, but loops wrapped around two warp threads. Each row of knots is followed by two weft shoots introduced from opposite directions.

Medieval Persian carpet weavers were inspired by numerous fine arts endeavors that were flourishing at the time. Manuscript illuminations, silk embroidery, miniature paintings, and metalwork all inspired the development of carpet design.

My own inspiration was a typical Tabriz medallion carpet with patterns in endless repeats of rosettes and palmettes. Carpet colors may range from bright and lively to dark and peaceful, with anywhere from two to twenty-eight different shades. I made do with nine! The richness of the colors in this bag design work in concert with the fine gauge to emulate the exquisite artistry unique to the Persian carpet.

Persian Carpet Bag

Persian Carpet bag

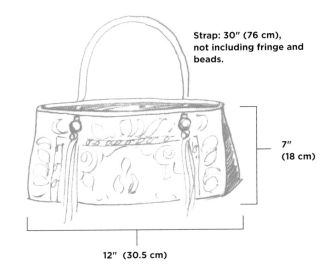

Strap: 30" (76 cm), not including fringe and beads.

7" (18 cm)

12" (30.5 cm)

FINISHED SIZE: 7" (18 cm) deep × 12" (30.5 cm) wide

YARN Rowan rowanspun 4 ply (100% pure new wool, 162 yd [148 m]/25 g). #708 midnight (A), #709 holly (B), #710 burgundy (C), #711 sludge (D), #706 reed (E), #705 spiced orange (F), #712 jade (G), #701 swarm (H), #702 stone (I). 1 hank of each color.

NEEDLES Size 3 (3.25 mm) circular (circ) 24" (61 cm)—bag body. Size 2 (2.75 mm) set of 2 double-pointed (dpn)—handle.

NOTIONS 2 large *Raku beads about 3" (7.5 cm) in circumference; tapestry needle; few yards of smooth cotton waste yarn to use as stitch holders and invisible (provisional) CO; stitch markers.

GAUGE 38 sts and 44 rows = 4" (10 cm) in stockinette stitch on larger needles.

NOTE *Raku is an Asian cracked-glaze firing technique; these beads are available at specialty bead shops.

NOTE Make increases using simple reverse loop cast on.

Center Rug With yarn H and circ needle, CO 70 sts. Work in St st, and follow Chart I for 110 rows, using a combination of intarsia and Fair Isle (see Techniques, pages 141 and 142). BO. Weave in ends and block piece for easy stitch pick up of borders. Let dry completely.

NOTE There are 2 short-side borders and 2 long-side borders. Instructions for each are numbered as follows: Short-side Border #1. Long-side Border #2. Short-side Border #3. Long-side Border #4. Additionally, there are 4 gussets, 2 attached to each long-side border. These are labeled as gusset half a, gusset half b, gusset half c, and gusset half d (see Figure A).

SHORT-SIDE BORDER #1 With yarn A and circ needle, pick up 70 sts across one short end of center rug (this is row 1 on Chart II). Follow Chart II, Rows 1–26.

At the same time, on Row 25 of chart work 2 one-row buttonholes as follows: K18, [yarn forward, slip next st purlwise, yarn back, *slip next st, then on right needle, BO 1 st; rep from * 3 times (4 sts BO), return last slipped st to left-hand needle, turn work. Take yarn to back, cable CO (see Techniques, page 140) 5 sts, turn work. Wyib (see Abbreviations, page 146) slip the first st from the left needle onto the right needle, and pass the extra CO st over it to

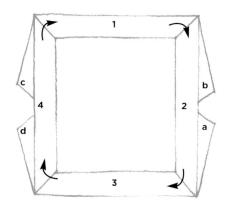

Figure A

close the buttonhole.] K48 sts; rep between [ ] to make another buttonhole, knit to end of row as shown on chart.

LONG-SIDE BORDER #2 With RS facing, move clockwise from first short-side border (see Figure A). Working along selvedge edge of center rug, using yarn A, pick up 106 sts, almost 1 st in each edge st (the picked-up sts are shown as Row 1 on Chart IIIa). Follow Chart IIIa, Rows 1–7, and using the same increase methods as were used on Short-side Border #1.

Row 3: Attach long-side border to short-side border as you knit the miter, working as follows: k1, inc 1, work across chart row until 1 st remains, inc 1, slip last st of long-side border on to the right-hand needle, with right needle insert the tip knitwise into the st edge on the right-hand side of Short-side Border #1, place this stitch on to the right-hand needle, and knit both sts tog through the front loops as if working an ssk. Complete Row 7 of Chart IIIa, but do not BO sts. Begin Chart IIIb, working Rows 8–25, making increases as shown on chart, and repeating miter joins every RS row.

*Row 26 (WS), **final row of long-side border.***Work turning ridge as follows: Mark center 16 sts; k56 sts, decreasing 4 sts evenly— (52 sts); purl BO center 16 sts; knit to end of row, decreasing 4 sts evenly—(52 sts rem on each side of BO). Turn. With RS facing, work the first 52 sts on needle as gusset half "a," placing the remaining 52 sts on stitch holder to use later as gusset half "b."

FIRST GUSSET HALF "a" *Row 1* (RS): With yarn A, k52 sts.

Row 2 and all even numbered rows: Work in k1, p1 rib to end of row, turn.

Row 3: BO 10 sts, work in rib until 3 sts rem, k2tog, work 1 st (41 sts).

Row 5: BO 10 sts, rib to end (31 sts).

Row 7: Same as for row 3 (20 sts).

Row 9: BO 10 sts, rib to end (10 sts).

Row 11: BO rem 10 sts, cut yarn and fasten off.

SECOND GUSSET HALF "b"

Row 1: With RS facing, attach yarn A at the left side of center BO, k52 sts turn.

Row 2 and all even numbered rows: BO 10 sts, work in k1, p1 rib to end of row—(42 sts).

Row 3: Work 1 st, work 2 sts tog, rib to end—(41sts).

Row 5: Work in rib.

Row 7: Rep Row 3–(20 sts)

Row 9: Rep Row 5.

Row 10: BO rem 10 sts.

SHORT-SIDE BORDER #3 Move work clockwise from Long-side Border #2, and repeat Short-side Border #1 instructions and Chart II, attaching mitered corner on all RS rows.

LONG-SIDE BORDER #4 Move work clockwise and work this border the same as Long-side Border #2, following Charts IIIa and b. Work instructions for gussets as

Knit on RS; purl on WS.

:: #708 midnight (A)   ▓ #710 burgundy (C)   – #706 reed (E)   ▲ #712 jade (G)   ◆ #702 stone (I)

|| #709 holly (B)   ◇ #711 sludge (D)   ○ #705 spiced orange (F)   □ #701 swarm (H)   □ pattern repeat box

Chart I Carpet Center

After completing Rows 1–55, continue rug center by working same chart from top to bottom, Rows 56–110, starting with a WS row.

end

begin

NOTE: Center Rug of the carpet bag is 110 rows in length. Work chart Rows 1–55, then work the chart from top to bottom beg with WS Row 56.

Chart II, Short-side Border

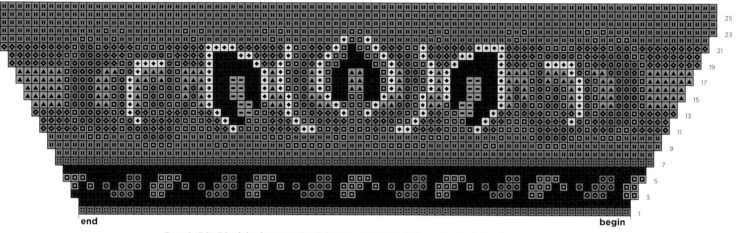

Row 1 (RS) 70 picked up sts. Work increase rows as follows: K1, inc 1 st using reverse loop CO, work across row to right before last st, inc 1, k1. Work buttonholes on Row 25 according to Short-side Border #1 instructions. Place all sts on yarn holder after completing Row 26 (WS).

Chart IIIa, Long-side Border, lower motif section

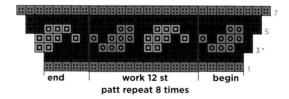

Row 1 (RS) is the 106 st pick up row.

NOTE: Work side increases using same method and placement as Short-side Border, Chart II.

*Row 3: Beg joining long-side border to short-side border as indicated in the long-side border instructions. After completing Row 7, do not BO. Complete long-side border by working Chart IIIb.

Chart IIIb Long-side Border

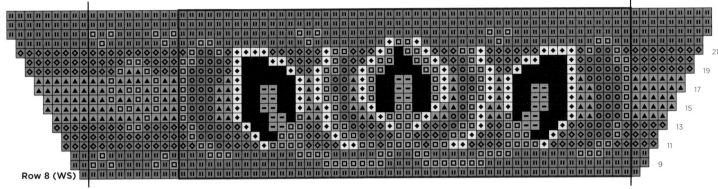

Row 8 (WS)

NOTE: Work all increases, and cont to join Long-side Border #2 to Short-side Border #1 the same as begun Chart IIIa. Follow Long-side Border #4 instructions when attaching to Short-side Border #3 (the second set of borders)

This chart begins with WS row (8), work as follows: Beg at left edge, purl across row to the black marker on the right side of chart once (61 sts on Row 8), then rep the 50 sts inside the red lines of the pattern repeat box, finish row by working remaining st(s) on far side of black marker—112 sts on needle in Row 8.

RS rows (Row 9 is first RS row): Beg at right edge, inc 1 st, knit across all sts up to the black marker on the left side of chart (62 sts), then rep 50 sts inside the red lines of patt rep box, finish row by working remaining st(s) on far side of black marker, inc 1 st in last st as shown on chart.

AT THE SAME TIME, cont joining long border to short border as begun in Chart IIIa, and working increases as established. After completing Row 25, return to Long-side Border #2 instructions for Row 26 instructions.

before, referring to gusset half "a" instructions to make gusset half "c," and referring to gusset half "b" instructions to make gusset half "d." Attach mitered corner at the beg of row to the left side of Short-side Border #1 as follows: With empty right needle, pick up a strand from the back on the left edge of Short-side Border #1, and place on left needle; knit this strand together with first stitch as if working k2tog.

LINING (work in stripes, see color suggestions below)
With yarn A and circ needle, CO 90 sts. Beg with RS row, work 2 rows in St st.
Row 3: Work one row buttonholes as follows: K17 sts, repeat buttonhole row instructions as for Short-side Border #1, beginning buttonhole instructions at [through knit to end.

At the same time, shape lining as follows: (see Figure B) Inc 1 stitch each end of row every ¾" (2 cm) 7 times—(104 sts). BO 3 sts at beg of next 2 rows, 2 sts at beg of next 4 rows—(90 sts). Work even for 1¾" (4.5 cm). Cable cast on (see Techniques, page 140) 2 sts at beg of next 4 rows, 3 sts at beg of next 2 rows—(104 sts). Dec 1 st each end of row every ¾" (2 cm) 7 times—(90 sts). Work buttonhole row ¼" (6 mm) *before* finishing the lining, and BO.

At the same time, work stripe pattern using the following colors (or as you wish! get creative!): 1½" (3.8 cm) yarn A; ¾" (2 cm) yarn G; ½" (1.3 cm) yarn E; ¾" (2 cm) yarn H; 2 rows yarn E; 4 rows yarn F; 2 rows yarn E; 2" (5 cm) yarn H; 4 rows yarn E; ½" (1.3 mm) yarn F—center bottom. Reverse order of color striping for second half of lining. BO all sts. With tapestry needle, weave loose ends to WS.

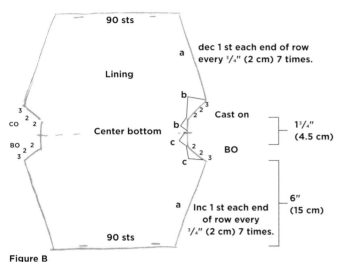

Figure B

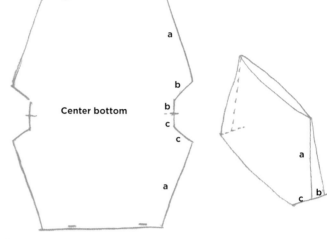

Figure C

HANDLE With dpn and 1 strand yarn A, 1 strand yarn B held together as one, CO 5 sts. *Wyib, sl 1 knitwise, [p1, k1] 2 times. Wyif (see Abbreviations, page 146), sl 1 purlwise, [k1, p1] 2 times*. Rep patt from * to * until piece measures 30" (76 cm), or desired length. BO. Block all pieces.

FINISHING Sew bag body and lining according to diagram (see Figure C). Place RS of bag body together, and with yarn threaded on tapestry needle, stitch sides "a" together using backstitch (see Techniques, page 139) for bag body. Place WS of lining together, and stitch sides together using invisible weaving seam for St st (see Techniques, page 142). Then fold bag body pieces to place RS together with "a" over center bottom mark, matching side b to b, and c to c as shown in Figure C. Sew these edges tog using backstitch. Work lining pieces the same. Fold bag body RS out.

ATTACHED I-CORD EDGE (see Techniques, page 139) Place bag edge sts held on waste yarn onto circ needle; beginning at side gusset seam using yarn C and waste yarn, CO 3 sts using invisible (provisional) CO (see Techniques, page 142). With yarn C, *k2, slip 2 knitwise (1 st from cord and 1 from bag edge), knit together as for ssk. Pass 3 sts back to left needle and rep from * until all sts along top edge of bag have been attached to I-cord. Remove waste yarn from CO; cut yarn leaving 6" (15 cm) tail, thread tapestry needle, and graft end of I-cord sts to beginning (see Techniques, page 143).

With WS of lining facing WS of body bag, whipstitch (see Techniques, page 145) top edge of lining to the inside of bag body, working just under I-cord on inside. Weave in all loose ends.

Handle: Thread ends of handle through buttonholes (see bag illustration on page 38). Cut 9 strands, each 16" (40.5 cm) long and in various colors, for each end of handle. With threaded tapestry needle, insert strands to the halfway point on end of handle. Fold strands down and thread all 18 through hole in bead. Tie strands in overhand knot to secure. Work other side of handle in the same way.

I n the north central region of Central Asia, the
carpets were woven solely by women. Uzbek
women also used their carpet-weaving skills to
create bags of various sizes and shapes. The
Uzbeks called the bags *napramach* and *karchin*, and
they hung them on the inside of the tent wall to
serve as containers for clothes and household uten-
sils. These bags included the long *aina khalta* for
mirrors; the round stitched *igsalik* for spindles; and
the *bukhcha* for books. Paintings from the nineteenth
century depict the beauty and complexity of these
marvelous textiles.

Uzbek carpet and bag designs are composed of
bands of geometric motifs or medallions. One or
more central medallions are surrounded by an
"open"—i.e., empty—field or partially filled with de-
tached small motifs. I was particularly taken with the
strength of the diagonals in the shapes of the individual motifs and in the overall compositions. My
bag design reflects Uzbek banded geometry and
their traditional palette, which was limited by available materials for natural dyes. Shades of reds were
used most frequently, blues and greens somewhat
less. By coloring identical design elements differently, I was able to create an impression of richness
with only six colors. I "frosted this cake" with compact, full tassels.

Napramach

Napramach

FINISHED SIZE 12″ (30.5 cm) deep × 9″ (23 cm) wide. 16″ (40.5 cm) deep from top opening to tip.

YARN Rowan felted tweed (50% merino wool, 25% alpaca, 25% viscose rayon, 191 yd [175 m]/50 g). #133 midnight (A), #144 conker (B), #141 whisper (C), #136 corn (D), #140 arctic (E), #145 treacle (F). 1 ball of each color.

NEEDLES Size 3 (3.25 mm)—bag body. Size 3 (3.25 mm) set of 2 double-pointed (dpn)—to use as temporary stitch holders. Adjust needle size if necessary to obtain the correct gauge.

NOTIONS Size D/3 (3.25 mm) crochet hook; tapestry needle; stitch markers; 2″ (5 cm) card or index card cut to size to use in making tassels.

GAUGE 26 sts and 24 rows = 4″ (10 cm) in stockinette stitch.

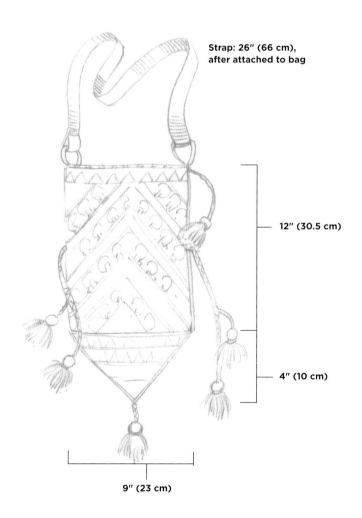

Strap: 26″ (66 cm), after attached to bag

12″ (30.5 cm)

4″ (10 cm)

9″ (23 cm)

NOTES

1. Use k1f&b increase on RS rows and p1f&b on WS rows.
2. The main body is worked from top to bottom, and begins as 2 separate triangles. Both triangles are later joined as one to complete the main body rectangle (see Figure A). The top border trim is worked after picking up sts across the main rectangle. The lower triangle is worked after picking up sts across lower edge of main rectangle. (See Figure B for complete directional layout.)

TOP TRIANGLE CORNER #1 With C, CO 2 sts. Follow Chart I, beg with purl foundation row (WS) as shown, then work rows 1 through 22—46 sts. Break yarn, place sts on spare dpn to hold.

TOP TRIANGLE CORNER #2 With C, CO 2 sts. Follow Chart II, beg with purl foundation row (WS), then work rows 1 through 22—46 sts. Break yarn, place sts on spare dpn to hold.

NOTE The main rectangle is worked from 2 charts. Follow Chart IIIa for the first half of RS rows, then follow

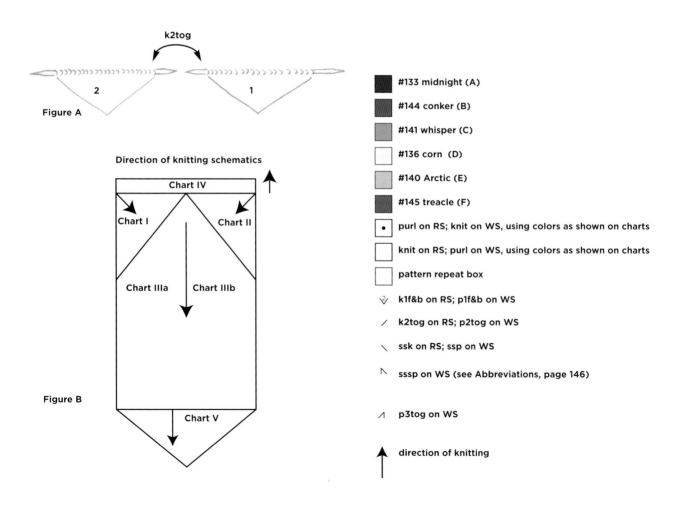

Figure A

Direction of knitting schematics

Figure B

#133 midnight (A)

#144 conker (B)

#141 whisper (C)

#136 corn (D)

#140 Arctic (E)

#145 treacle (F)

· purl on RS; knit on WS, using colors as shown on charts

knit on RS; purl on WS, using colors as shown on charts

pattern repeat box

k1f&b on RS; p1f&b on WS

k2tog on RS; p2tog on WS

ssk on RS; ssp on WS

sssp on WS (see Abbreviations, page 146)

p3tog on WS

direction of knitting

Chart I

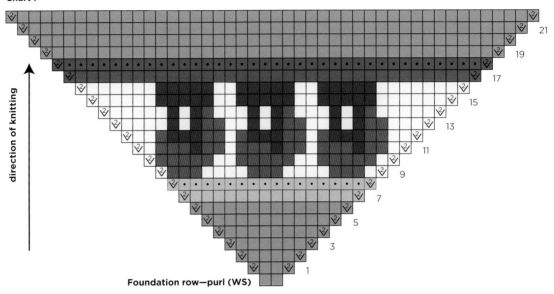

direction of knitting

Foundation row—purl (WS)

21
19
17
15
13
11
9
7
5
3
1

Chart II

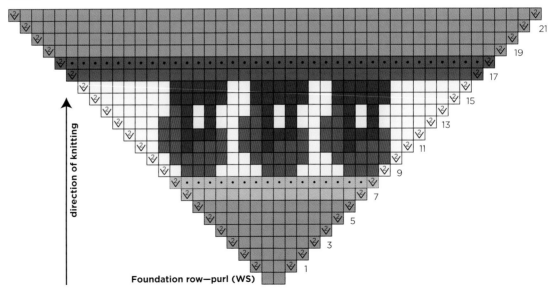

direction of knitting

Foundation row—purl (WS)

21
19
17
15
13
11
9
7
5
3
1

Chart IIIb to complete the RS row. On WS rows, follow Chart IIIb for the first half of row, and then work Chart IIIa to complete the WS row.

MAIN RECTANGLE

Join both triangles: (see Figure A) Using main needles and C, begin Chart IIIa with Row 23, working as follows: (RS) k1f&b at right edge, knit across sts of corner triangle #1 up to the last st, place marker (pm) before last st, k2tog, (this will be last st of triangle #1 worked together with first st of triangle #2), pm; move to Chart IIIb and work Row 23 as shown to complete row—93 sts.

Continue working increases, decreases, and motifs from both charts until Row 78 is complete. Work final 3 sts as: Sl 1, k2tog, psso (see Abbreviations, page 146). Break yarn and pull through rem st to secure. Weave in loose ends to WS. Make second side of bag to match.

Steam block rectangles to make them easier to work borders and finishing. Dry completely.

TOP BORDER

With F, and RS facing, pick up 60 sts along top of mitered bag rectangle (60 sts shown as Row 1 on Chart IV). Work Chart IV, Rows 1–10, then BO on Row 11 using 2-color BO (see Techniques, page 139) in colors A and D. Repeat for other mitered bag rectangle.

LOWER EDGE TRIANGLE

With color F, pick up 60 sts along bottom edge of bag (shown as Row 1 on Chart V). Begin Chart V working Rows 1–32. Finish final 2 sts as k2tog, cut yarn and pull through rem st. Repeat for second triangle. Weave in all ends and steam block. Let dry completely.

FINISHING

With crochet hook and A, chain 13 (see Techniques for basic crochet sts, page 140). *Skip first chain from hook and single crochet into each chain*; do not break yarn (first strap loop made). Pin WS of bag together and on the RS of work single crochet around the side and bottom edges. Work 2 single crochet into 1 st at outside corners, and 3 single crochet into bottom point; do not break yarn. Chain 13 and rep from * to *, making the second strap loop. Break yarn leaving an 8" (20.5 cm) tail. With yarn tail threaded on tapestry needle, sew loop ends securely to WS at top edge.

STRAP

With A, CO 7 sts. [With yarn in front, sl 1 purl-wise, yarn back, knit to end.]

Repeat instructions between [ ] until strap measures 28" (71 cm) unstretched. BO. Insert one end of strap into crocheted loop and fold it upward about 1" (2.5 cm), backstitch (see Techniques, page 139) across strap end to secure. Attach other end in the same manner.

BRAID CORDS AND TASSELS

Cut three 36" (91.5 cm) strands, 1 each of colors A, B, and D. At midpoint on the side edge of main body rectangle, insert the strands to halfway—(18") [46 cm]. Using 2 strands of each color, braid together for 7" (18 cm), tie overhand knot to secure.

Tassel: Make tassel using B, wrapping yarn 50 times around a 2" (5 cm) card. Cut one side of strands and lay them over the knot at the braid end. Tie ends of braid in square knot around tassel strands. Tie 2 strands of B around tassel head and wrap several times, tie square knot to secure. Thread B tassel wrap ends on tapestry needle and insert into center of tassel and out at the bottom. Cut longest ends, but do not trim tassel strands—leave them slightly uneven.

Midpoint braid: Work a second braid at the midpoint of first braid as follows: Cut 12" (30.5 cm) strands of A, B, and D, one strand of each color. Insert the strands to halfway (6") [15 cm] into first braid. Braid these strands

Chart IIIb

No repeat boxes on Rows 65–78
actual stitch count as shown for
Chart IIIb.

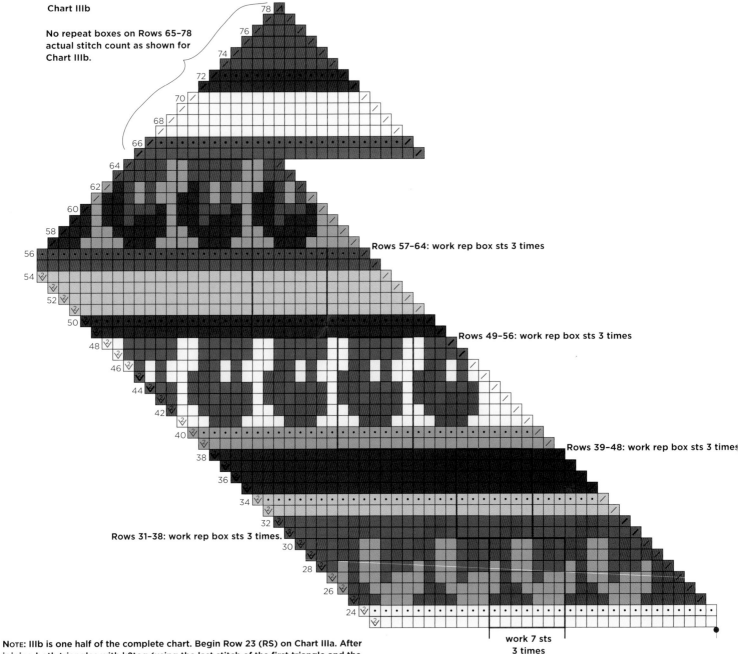

Rows 57–64: work rep box sts 3 times

Rows 49–56: work rep box sts 3 times

Rows 39–48: work rep box sts 3 times

Rows 31–38: work rep box sts 3 times.

work 7 sts
3 times

NOTE: IIIb is one half of the complete chart. Begin Row 23 (RS) on Chart IIIa. After joining both triangles with k2tog (using the last stitch of the first triangle and the first st of the second triangle, and shown as center st on Chart IIIa), beg this chart at the right edge, place marker, knit across to last st in row, k1f&b—93 sts on needle.

Row 24: (WS) K1f&b, knit to red marker, slip marker, move to Chart IIIa and follow Row 24 on that chart to finish. When Row 24 is completed, the total number of sts on needle is 95 sts, and remains at 95 sts until Row 57, when decreases begin on both edges to shape the bottom edge of the bag. Slip markers each side of center st on every row. Check your stitch count frequently.

Chart IIIa

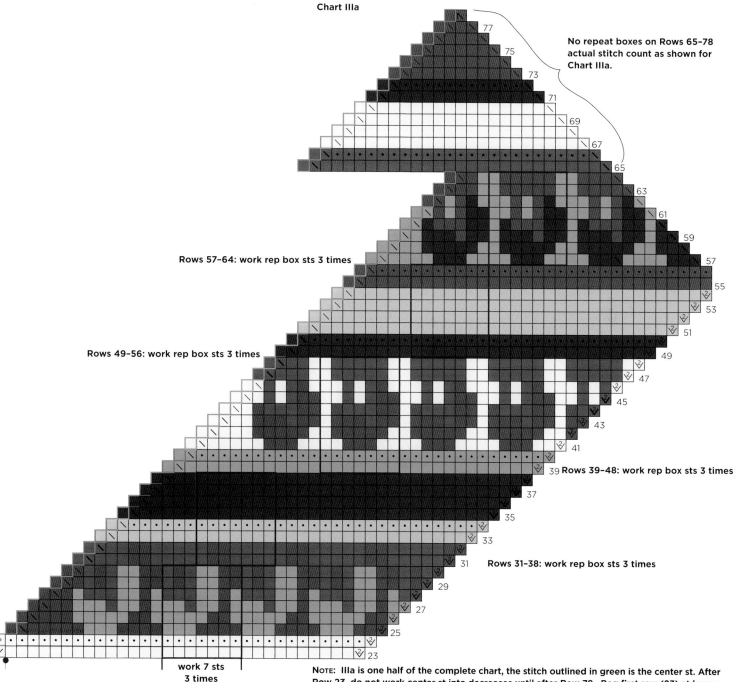

No repeat boxes on Rows 65-78 actual stitch count as shown for Chart IIIa.

77
75
73
71
69
67
65

63
61
59
57
55
53
51

Rows 57-64: work rep box sts 3 times

49
47
45
43
41
39 Rows 39-48: work rep box sts 3 times

Rows 49-56: work rep box sts 3 times

37
35
33 Rows 31-38: work rep box sts 3 times
31
29
27
25
23

work 7 sts
3 times

NOTE: IIIa is one half of the complete chart, the stitch outlined in green is the center st. After Row 23, do not work center st into decreases until after Row 78. Beg first row (23) at lower right side with k1f&b, knit to last st, place marker, k2tog (using the last stitch of the first triangle and the first st of the second triangle). Move to Chart IIIb, place marker, knit across to last st, k1f&b—93 sts total. On RS rows work across Row to 2 sts before the center st, make the decrease, slip marker, work center st, move to Chart IIIb, slip marker, work the beg decrease, knit rem sts as shown, ending row with k1f&b. After Row 24 (WS) is completed, the total # of sts on needle is 95 sts, and remains at 95 sts until Row 57, when decreases begin on both edges to shape the bottom edge of the bag. After Row 78, work final 3 sts as: Sl 1, k2tog, psso, cut yarn and pull through rem st to secure. Check stitch count frequently.

for 2" (5 cm), tying overhand knot to secure, and finishing end with a tassel made in color D and wrapped with color B. Repeat for other side of rectangle, first tassel in A, wrapped with B, second tassel in D, wrapped with A.

Bottom point braid: Cut 12" (30.5 cm) strands using same colors as before. Work braid for 1" (2.5 cm) and finish as above, making tassel in A, wrapped with B.

Top corner braid: Cut 24" (61 cm) strands for braid, follow the same process as before, making tassel in E, wrapped with D. Weave in loose ends to WS of work.

Chart IV—top border

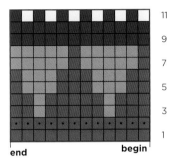

Row 1 is the 60-st pick-up row.
Row 11 is the 2-color BO row.

Chart V—lower edge triangle

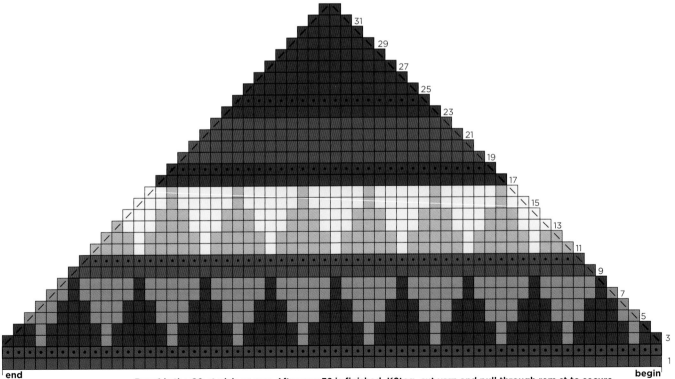

Row 1 is the 60-st pick-up row. After row 32 is finished, K2tog, cut yarn and pull through rem st to secure.

On the eastern periphery of the Persian Empire, Tajikistan lies between Uzbekistan to the north and Afghanistan to the south. Situated along the ancient Silk Road trade route between China and Persia, it naturally developed markets to provide tea and silk to Middle Eastern cultures. Teahouses were popular social gathering places for sharing news and food.

Fortunately, I didn't have to go far to experience an authentic Tajik teahouse since a complete one was dismantled and shipped from the Tajik city of Dushanbe and reconstructed in its sister city of Boulder, Colorado, in 1998. Teahouse design is intended to recall a walled garden which, for the Tajiks, is a symbol of paradise. When I entered the Boulder teahouse, it felt as if I truly *had* found a slice of paradise. The folk architecture of this building is carved and painted with stylized floral and plant motifs. The ornate patterns are lavish and colorful: bright blues, cool apple greens, cheerful pinks.

Keeping my color scheme simple, I chose to highlight the apple green and contrast it with a cobalt blue. The sheen of the yarn offers the same flavor as the gloss of the painted surfaces. I embellished the knitted fabric with curvilinear designs using a chain stitch crochet similar to that which I once saw on a Tajik scarf.

Tea House
Sling Bag & Coin Purse

FINISHED SIZE 8½″ (21.5 cm) deep x 10″ (25.5 cm) wide, 23″ (58.5 cm) total length including strap.

YARN Classic Elite Provence (100% mercerized cotton, 256 yd [234 m]/100 g).

#2681 bright chartreuse green (MC), 2 hanks. #2657 DeNimes blue, 1 hank (CC).

NEEDLES Size 3 (3.25 mm) set of 4 or 5 double-pointed (dpn) or 16″ (40.5 cm) circular (circ)—bag body. Size 3 (3.25 mm)—1 pair for 3-needle BO. Adjust needle size if necessary to obtain the correct gauge.

NOTIONS Size D/3 (3.25 mm) crochet hook; tapestry needle; stitch holder; water-erasable marker—available at fabric store; few yards of smooth waste yarn for invisible (provisional) CO and to use as stitch holder; 1 button ⅝″ (1.5 cm) for coin purse.

GAUGE 24 sts and 36 rows = 4″ (10 cm) in stockinette stitch, a very snug gauge.

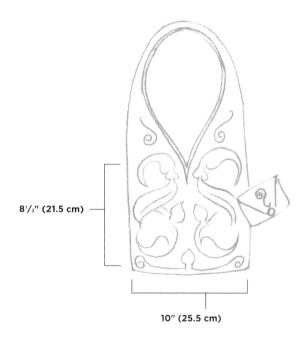

8½″ (21.5 cm)

10″ (25.5 cm)

NOTE Use M1L and M1R increases (see Techniques, page 143) unless other inc methods are specified.

STRAP With MC and waste yarn, CO 15 sts using invisible (provisional) CO (see Techniques, page 142) method. With MC, work in St st until piece measures 6" (15 cm).

Next RS row: Increase as follows: K1, M1R, knit across row until 1 st remains, M1L, k1. Rep inc every 6th row 1 time, every 4th row 2 times, every other row 14 times, every 4th row 2 times, every 6th row 2 times—(59 sts— 63 rows). Work 5 more rows, ending RS facing. Place sts on holder. Make a second strap same, but keep these sts on needle.

BAG BODY (work in the round to bottom) Using dpn or 16" (40.5 cm) circ needles, knit across 58 sts on needles, k1f&b (see Abbreviations, page 146) in next st—(60 sts) followed immediately by knitting the 59 sts on holder working k1f&b in last st—120 sts. Knit 30 sts, place marker (m). This m indicates a side "seam" for later finishing. Work St st in the rnd until piece measures 8½" (21.5 cm) from join, ending at m. Place all sts onto waste yarn long enough to smooth out knitting in preparation for embroidery. Work embroidery before completing bag body.

Figure A

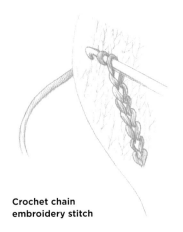

Crochet chain embroidery stitch

Figure B

Figure C

EMBELLISHMENT Enlarge design (see Techniques, page 141) and transfer onto bag using erasable marker. With CC and crochet hook, embroider the design (see Figures A, B) on both sides of bag using crochet chain stitch as follows: With RS facing, and holding working yarn on WS, insert crochet hook into knitted fabric, wrap working yarn over the hook and draw up a loop through knitted fabric to RS. *Following design line, insert hook into next appropriate spot, wrap yarn over hook and draw up a new loop through the knitted fabric and through the loop on crochet hook; rep from * until design is finished. Turn direction, and start in a new area as needed. To secure the last chain st, cut working yarn, leaving an 8" (20.5 cm) tail. Wrap yarn over hook and pull yarn tail through to the RS. Thread tail on tapestry needle and insert to WS at the top of the last chain st. Work in all ends on WS to secure. Avoid pulling chain sts too tightly to prevent puckering the knitting.

Complete bag body as follows: Turn bag inside out. Remove sts from waste yarn, placing 60 sts on each of 2 straight needles, with points facing the side marker. Work 3-needle BO (see Techniques, page 139) for a secure stable lower edge.

Join strap ends: Remove waste yarn from CO edges, and with MC threaded on tapestry needle, graft strap sts together using Kitchener st (see Techniques, page 142). Block bag.

FINISHING With CC and crochet hook, single crochet (see Techniques, page 144) around each strap edge. Turn inside corner by working first half of single crochet into 3 consecutive sts (4 loops on hook), then draw a loop through all loops on hook.

STITCH GUIDE FOR COIN PURSE
Seed stitch: (2 st rep; + 1)
All rows: *K1, p1; rep from * to last st, k1.

COIN PURSE With MC, CO 25 sts. Work seed stitch for 3 rows. Begin St st and work even until piece measures 6" (15 cm).

Shape flap:
Row 1: P1, ssk, (see Abbreviations, page 146) knit across row until 3 sts remain, k2tog, p1.
Row 2: P1, k1, purl to last 2 sts, k1, p1. Repeat last 2 rows until 7 sts remain. With RS facing, P1, k1, work one-row buttonhole (see Techniques, page 144) over next 3 sts, then p1 to end row.
Next row (WS): [P1, k2tog] 2 times, p1—(5 sts rem) BO in patt.

Work swirl design (see Figure C) on flap using crochet chain stitch embroidery (see Embellishment section, left). Mark button placement and sew on button. Weave in all loose ends to WS.

Afghanistan

Afghanistan is a land of great mountains, scorching deserts, fertile valleys, and rolling plains in the eastern region of Central Asia. In a tradition that flourished hundreds of years ago, and is still pursued by a small number of tribes today, nomads roamed the grasslands with their herds of livestock. They lived in camel hair tents, called *yurts*, and their decorative arts were necessarily portable. They stored their possessions in woven and knotted bags, often of magnificent workmanship and design. These bags were hung on the inside of the yurt or placed on the ground as a cushion. Afghan nomads also adorned their camels, horses, and donkeys with woven trappings, including *eyerlik* (saddle cloth) and *khurjin* (saddlebags).

For this project, the simple bag shape was my canvas, the warm, dark colors of the yarn were my paint, and the basic geometric patterns became the background for the fringes and tassels that I focused on as a visual statement. All these elements are part of Afghan textile art. And no Afghan inspired piece would be complete without the blue beads, which are meant to be a talisman against bad luck, to "ward off the evil eye."

Camel
Bag

Camel Bag

FINISHED SIZE 12″ (30.5 cm) deep x 11″ (28 cm) wide.

YARN Mission Falls 1824 Wool (100% merino superwash, 85 yd [78 m]/50 g). #17 heath (A), #24 damson (B). 1 ball each color. #10 russet (C), #30 teal (D). 2 balls each color.

NEEDLES Size 4 (3.5 mm). Adjust needle size if necessary to obtain the correct gauge.

NOTIONS Size D/3 (3.25 mm) crochet hook; 12 blue beads ½″ (1.3 cm), with holes big enough to insert 4 strands of yarn; stitch markers; tapestry needle; long straight sewing pins with colored heads.

GAUGE 22 sts and 28 rows = 4″ (10 cm) in stockinette stitch.

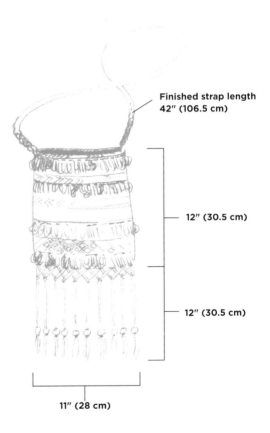

Finished strap length
42″ (106.5 cm)

12″ (30.5 cm)

12″ (30.5 cm)

11″ (28 cm)

STITCH GUIDE

Loop stitch row: (see Figure A in Dragon Ysgrepan, page 80)

Work loop stitch on chart Rows 11, 37, 65, and 83 as follows:

RS [K1, make loop: Knit into st; leave on left needle; yarn forward and draw around thumb, making a loop about 1½" (3.8 cm) long; yarn back and knit into st again, slipping st off left needle. Pass first st made over second and off end of needle]; rep between [ ] to end of row. Pull down on loops while they are still on needle to tighten knots.

BAG BODY

(worked from bottom to top in St st) With A, CO 62 sts. Purl foundation row (WS). Beg chart with Row 1 on RS. Work 2-color BO on Row 85 (see Techniques, page 139). Make second side to match.
Block pieces.

With B and WS tog, single crochet (see Techniques, page 144) around sides and bottom of bag, working 3 single crochet into each lower corner.

FRINGE

(see Figure A) Cut 24 strands of B, each 30" (76 cm) long. Using long straight sewing pins as markers, insert markers along bottom edge of bag at 1" (2.5 cm) intervals—12 markers. Insert 2 strands of B to halfway (15") [38 cm] at each marker. Secure each set of strands with fringe knots (see Figure A), using tapestry needle in knot to force knot to lie snugly against bottom edge—4 strands hang from each knot. Take 2 strands from each knot and lay them so they're angled to the right. Take remaining 2 strands from each knot and lay them over the top of the first strands, angling them to the left. Extreme side ends should hang straight down. Where strands meet and cross, tie overhand knot 2" (5 cm) down from bottom edge of bag. Tie overhand knots in each 4-strand fringe 5" (12.5 cm) down from the second knots. Thread a bead onto each and tie last overhand knots to secure.

STRAP

Cut 2 strands of A and 4 strands B each 90" (228.5 cm) long. Insert all strands under 2-color BO to halfway (45") [114.5 cm] at side edge of bag. Make braid using 3 sets of 4 strands each until strap measures 42" (106.5 cm), or desired length. Tie other end of strap under 2-color BO on opposite side edge of bag. Leave fringed ends of strap on inside of bag.

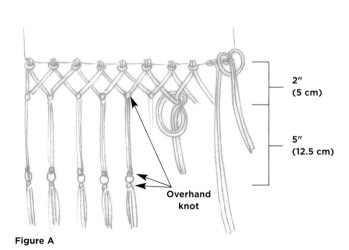

2"
(5 cm)

5"
(12.5 cm)

Overhand knot

Figure A

Knit on RS; purl on WS.
Work loop st on rows as indicated, following instructions given in Stitch Guide.

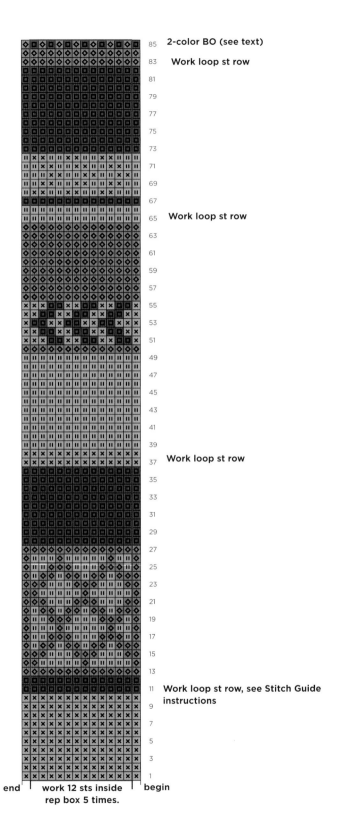 #17 heath (A)	
#24 damson (B)	
#10 russet (C)	
#30 teal (D)	
patt rep box	

85 2-color BO (see text)
83 Work loop st row
81
79
77
75
73
71
69
67
65 Work loop st row
63
61
59
57
55
53
51
49
47
45
43
41
39
37 Work loop st row
35
33
31
29
27
25
23
21
19
17
15
13
11 Work loop st row, see Stitch Guide instructions
9
7
5
3
1

end   work 12 sts inside   begin
rep box 5 times.

CENTRAL ASIA

Turkey

Turkey occupies the western area of Central Asia around the Black Sea. To this day, Turkish nomads make their lives more comfortable and liven up their tent homes with vivid splashes of color in their textiles, from carpets to wall hangings to bags.

Kilim is the Turkish term for a pileless flatweave textile handwoven by tapestry techniques. In most kilims, a slit occurs wherever two colors meet along a vertical pattern line, but sometimes interlocking methods are employed to minimize these slits.

Before the nineteenth century, most kilim weaving was done by girls and women between the ages of fourteen and twenty-six who formed a special community within each neighborhood of the village; they moved fluidly in and out of each other's homes with no need to knock. They came to visit and to weave. The older women taught kilim weaving to the younger women, who then matured into a mastery of the art, creating designs full of innovation and surprises. Each unique element of a weaver's design would be a *hatra*, or a memento of girlhood friendships and events. These memories became an integral part of the kilim, which would be added to the weaver's dowry collection of beautiful things.

I could not overlook the dynamic and bold geometric designs of kilim carpets in my creative trek. I found the designs to be an intricate matrix of strong angles, points, and straight lines. My design evolved from looking at a myriad of carpets and then choosing colors that appear to have softened over time. I used reverse stockinette specifically to capture the surface texture of the typical kilim.

Kilim
Carpet Bag

FINISHED SIZE 9½" (24 cm) deep × 15½" (39.5 cm) wide.

YARN Mission Falls 1824 Cotton (100% cotton, 84 yd [77 m]/50 g). #100 black (MC), 3 balls. #402 sea (A), #304 moss (B), #204 lentil (C), #208 merlot (D). 1 ball of each color.

NEEDLES Size 4 (3.5 mm). Adjust needle size if necessary to obtain the correct gauge.

NOTIONS 8 blue beads ½" (1.3 cm), with holes big enough for 6 strands of yarn;

4 large bobby pins; tapestry needle.

GAUGE 20 sts and 26 rows = 4" (10 cm) in reverse stockinette stitch.

STITCH GUIDE
Reverse St st
Purl on RS rows, knit on WS rows.

NOTE Work bag in reverse St st intarsia (see Techniques, page 142). When you're changing colors over another color stitch, knit that st on the RS to make a clean color change.

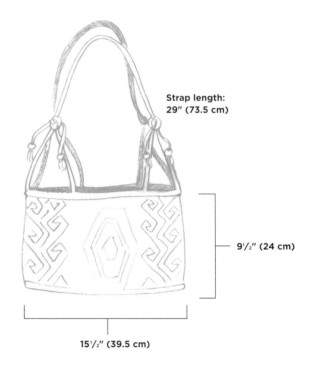

Strap length: 29" (73.5 cm)

9½" (24 cm)

15½" (39.5 cm)

Reverse St st: Purl on RS; knit on WS

□ #100 black (MC)   ☒ #304 moss (B)   ◆ #208 merlot (D)

+ #402 sea (A)   ‖ #204 lentil (C)

end   begin

BAG BODY With MC, CO 70 sts. (RS) Purl 1 row. Knit 1 row. Begin chart working Rows 1–66. After chart Row 66 is finished, change to MC and complete bag side as follows: Knit 2 rows. Purl 1 row. Knit 1 row. BO in purl. Make second side of bag to match. Block pieces and let dry completely.

FINISHING With WS tog, sew side seams using invisible weaving (see Techniques, page 142) for garter st.

Turn bag inside out, and with RS tog, seam bottom edge using slip stitch crochet (see Techniques, page 145). Weave in all ends on WS, turn bag right side out and begin handles.

BRAID HANDLES With MC, cut 6 strands, each 48" (122 cm) long. Insert strands to halfway (24") [61 cm] into top right corner of bag side. Braid 3 sets of 4 strands each for 6" (15 cm). Place bobby pin over braid to hold temporarily. Cut another 6 strands the same length as before. Mark top border of bag 3½" (9 cm) toward center of bag and repeat braid process at that mark. Remove bobby pins and tie all 24 strands in overhand knot. Continue with 12 strands, braid with 3 sets of 4 strands to end of strand lengths, place bobby pin to hold. With remaining 12 strands, make 2 braids, 3 sets of 2 strands each, 4" (10 cm) long. Thread a bead onto each short braid (as shown in photo) and tie overhand knot under bead. Trim strands to 1" (2.5 cm).

Repeat entire process at top left corner of bag, then flip bag to other side and repeat again. Take all 4 braids held with pins and tie overhand knot close to the top (shoulder) end, trim strands to 1" (2.5 cm).

Like a fairy tale, Ireland is enchanting, with its fine mist, ancient castles, thatch-roofed cottages, and low stone walls that enclose fields of the richest green. But one thing is certainly real: the warm hospitality of the Irish. This fascinating land's legacy to knitters is the stunning off-white, texturally complex, handknitted sweaters that orginated on Ireland's Aran Islands (off the west coast) around 1920. The Aran sweater is an artistic arrangement of a variety of stitches with names like the cable, the anchor, the basket, the honeycomb, the Celtic knot, and Jacob's ladder. Each stitch is tied to images of Celtic antiquities, Irish religious heritage, and the fishing industry that is so important to Ireland's livelihood.

The Irish influence comes through clearly in my two bag designs. In Irish Cables, the rope cable is reminiscent of fishing and the sea and the diamond is a Celtic symbol of wealth.

For the first bag I chose a color frequently seen in Ireland's landscape, the gray-brown of stone castle walls. This color is expressed beautifully in the wonderfully textured tweedy single-ply yarn. The natural color and basketweave stitch on the second bag, the Fish Creel, pay homage to the color used in Aran sweaters and to the fisherman who daily uses this fascinatingly shaped basket to hold his catch.

Irish
Cables

Irish Cables

FINISHED SIZE 12″ (30.5 cm) deep × 10″ (25.5 cm) wide.

YARN Tahki Donegal Tweed (100 % pure new wool, 183yd [168 m]/100 g). #868 camel grey, 2 hanks.

NEEDLES Size 4 (3.5 mm). Adjust needle size if necessary to obtain the correct gauge.

NOTIONS 2 buttons 1″ (2.5 cm) in diameter; cable needle; tapestry needle; 4 stitch markers (m); safety pin.

GAUGE 16 stitches and 28 rows = 4″ (10 cm) in seed stitch.

STITCH GUIDE
Seed st (even number of sts)
Row 1: *K1, p1; rep to end of row.
Row 2: *P1, k1; rep to end of row.
Rep Rows 1 and 2 for pattern.

NOTE For increases shown on chart: Use backward loop CO (see Techniques, page 140).

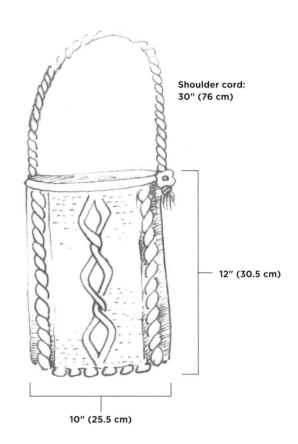

Shoulder cord: 30″ (76 cm)

12″ (30.5 cm)

10″ (25.5 cm)

BAG BODY CO 4 sts and work I-cord edge as follows: [K4, turn. K1, yarn forward, sl 3 sts purlwise, turn]. Rep instructions between [ ] until I-cord edge measures 10" (25.5 cm). End with right side facing. Work last row as: K4, pass first 3 sts over last st and off needle—1 st rem. Pick up 45 sts along garter edge—46 sts. When picking up, insert needle under full stitch (2 strands) so garter st edge is fully covered.

Foundation row: (WS) K1,*k1f&b, p6, k1f&b* (see Abbreviations, page 146), work 28 sts in seed st; rep from * to *, end k1—50 sts. Begin chart, increasing on Row 1 as shown, and placing markers as shown. Work Rows 1–82 for first side of bag. After Row 82, rep chart rows as instructed for second side of bag.

Top edge, second side: Work I-cord edge as follows: Cable CO (see Techniques, page 140) 3 sts. *K2, ssk (1 st from cord and 1 st from bag), slip 3 sts back to left needle; repeat from * until all sts of top edge are joined to I-cord, and only

3 sts of I-cord remain. Pass second and third sts over first and off end of needle. Cut yarn and pull through loop to secure.

FINISHING Fold bag in half lengthwise at bobbles (Row 79, side 1), and with WS tog sew invisible garter st seam (see Techniques, page 142) from right side of work. Weave in all loose ends to WS.

SHOULDER CORD Cut 10 strands, each 80" (203 cm) long. Tie all strands tog in a slipknot close to one end. Secure this end with a safety pin to your ironing board. With all strands held tog and pulled out to tension, twist yarn until when let slack it twists back on itself. When fully twisted, fold yarn in half and allow it to twist back on itself. Release slipknot from ironing board, and tie ends tog to secure cord. Clip to ½" (1.3 cm). Sew one button at each side of bag ½" (1.3 cm) from top edge, and slip each end of cord over buttons.

M   Inc 1 st by making a backward loop CO.

☐   Knit on RS; purl on WS

·   Purl on RS; knit on WS

✓   K2tog

☐   pattern repeat box

▨   no stitch

●   Bobble: (k1, yo, k1, yo, k1) into next st, turn,
    (p5, turn, k5, turn) 2 times. P2tog, p1, p2tog tbl,
    turn, sl 1, k2tog, psso.

●   marker

2/1 PLC: sl 2 sts onto cn and hold in front, p1, k2 from cn.

2/1 PRC: sl 1 st onto cn and hold in back, k2, p1 from cn

2/2 LC: sl 2 sts onto cn and hold in front; k2, k2 from cn.

slip next 3 sts onto cn and hold in back, k3, k3 from cn.

slip next 3 sts onto cn and hold in front, k3, k3 from cn.

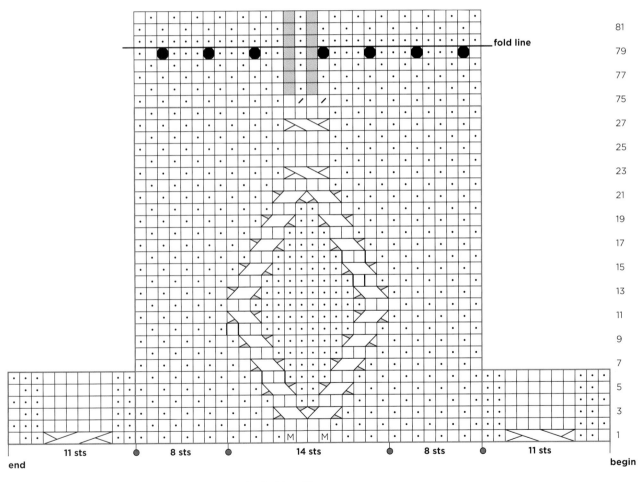

NOTE: Work first and last 11 sts in pattern throughout for both sides of bag.
Side 1: Work Rows 1–28 once; then Rows 3–28 once; then Rows 3–22 once—3 diamonds,
       74 rows. Cont chart at Row 75 through Row 79 (bobbles).
Side 2: Work Rows 80–82. Then work 74 rows the same as side 1, and finishing 3 diamonds.
       Complete side 2 working Rows 75 and 76. See instructions for final edging around top.

Irish
Creel

Irish Creel

FINISHED SIZE 8″ (20.5 cm) deep × 11″ (28 cm) wide.

YARN Reynolds Candide (100% Virgin Wool, 194 yd [177.5 m]/4 oz). #01 natural (MC), 2 hanks. #100 light grey heather (A), 1 hank.

NEEDLES Size 6 (4 mm)—bag body. Size 6 (4 mm) set of 2 double-pointed (dpn)—strap and I-cord. Adjust needle size if necessary to obtain the correct gauge.

NOTIONS 2 buttons, 1″ (2.5 cm) in diameter; tapestry needle; cable needle; long straight sewing pins with colored heads; few yards of smooth waste yarn for invisible (provisional) CO—strap.

GAUGE 29 sts and 23 rows = 4″ (10 cm) in basketweave st. A very stiff gauge.

STITCH GUIDE

Basketweave stitch (multiple of 2)

Row 1: (RS) K1, [knit into back of second st, then into front of first st, slip old sts off needle], end k1.

Row 2: P2, [purl into the front of second st, then into front of first st, slip old sts off needle], end p2.

C4B Cable:

Cable row: P1, place next 2 sts on to cable needle, hold in back, k2, k2 from cable needle (C4B), p1.

Rows 2 and 4: (WS) K1, p4, k1.

Row 3: P1, k4, p1.

Rep above 4 rows for patt.

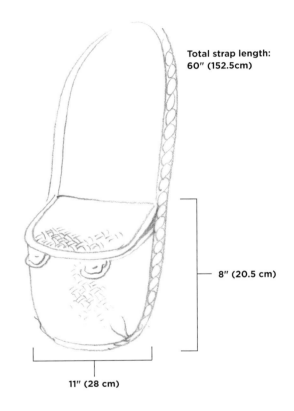

Total strap length: 60″ (152.5cm)

8″ (20.5 cm)

11″ (28 cm)

NOTE Use simple backward loop CO (see Techniques, page 140) as increases, unless other inc methods are specified.

BACK With MC, CO 36 sts. Purl 1 foundation row.

Row 1: K1, inc 1, [knit into back of second st, then into front of first st, slip old sts off needle]; rep [ ] to last st, inc 1, k1.

Row 2: P1, inc 1, [purl into front of second st, then into front of first st, slip old sts off needle]; rep between [ ] to last st, inc 1, p1.

Repeat last 2 rows until 66 sts on needle. Work even until piece measures 5½" (14 cm) from CO.

NOTE To keep continuity of pattern, the sts to be twisted will have to alternate, so as you increase or decrease sts, the number knitted or purled plain before twisting will change.

Decrease row: K1, ssk, work basketweave patt to last 3 sts, k2tog, k1—64 sts.
Work even until piece measures 7" (18 cm) from CO edge. Work second decrease row as: SSK, k1, work in basketweave until 3 sts rem, k1, k2tog—62 sts. Cont in basketweave patt until work measures 8½" (21.5 cm), end with RS facing.
Next row: K1, [k1, k2tog] 20 times, ending k1—42 sts.

Turning ridge: [On WS of work, knit 1 row. Purl 1 row] 2 times.
Next row: (WS) K1, *k1, k1f&b, (see Abbreviations, page 146); rep from * ending row with k1—62 sts. Work even in basketweave patt until piece measures 1" (2.5 cm) from last row of turning ridge.
Increase row: (RS) Inc 1 st at beg and end of row. Work even in patt until piece measures 2" (5 cm) from turning ridge, then rep increase row. When piece measures 3" (7.5 cm) from last row of turning ridge, begin 4 decrease rows working as follows: (RS) [SSK at beg of row, work in basketweave to last 2 sts, k2tog.
Next row: P2tog at beg of row, work in basketweave to last 2 sts, ssp (see Abbreviations, page 146)] work between [ ] 2 times—58 sts. BO in patt.

FRONT With MC, CO 60 sts. Purl 1 row. Work next 4 rows as follows: Cable CO 7 sts (see Techniques, page 140), work in basketweave to end, turn—88 sts.
Next 8 rows: Inc 1 st each end of row—104 sts. Work even in basketweave until piece measures 5" (12.5 cm) from CO.

Decrease row: Dec 1 st at beg and end of row. Work dec row again at 6" (15 cm), and at 7" (18 cm)—98 sts.

Shape upper curve: (RS) Work 20 sts in basketweave, BO 58 sts in patt, work rem sts in basketweave—(20 sts each side of BO). Working yarn is attached to left side only, turn.
Next row: (WS) Work in basketweave to last st, turn.
Next row: (RS) With 1 st on right needle, slip first st from left needle to right, BO 1 st, BO 5 more in patt, basketweave to end—14 sts.
Next row: Work 13 sts in basketweave, turn.
Next row: With 1 st on right needle, slip first st from left needle to right, BO 1 st, then BO 5 more in patt, work basketweave to end—8 sts.
Next row: Work 7 sts in basketweave, turn.
Next row: With 1 st on right needle, slip first st, BO 1 st, BO 3 more in patt, work basketweave to end—4 sts.
Next row: P3, turn. BO rem sts. With WS facing, join MC at the first st of the 20 sts (next to BO sts), and shape right upper curve to match: slip 1 from left needle to right, p1, BO 1 st, BO 5 more in patt, work basketweave to end—14 sts.
Next row: (RS) Work 13 sts in basketweave, turn.
Next row: With 1 st on right needle, slip first st from left needle to right, BO 1 st, BO 5 more in patt, basketweave to end—8 sts.
Next row: Work 7 sts in basketweave, turn.
Next row: With 1 st on right needle, slip first st from left needle, BO 1 st, BO 3 more in patt, basketweave to end—4 sts.
Next row: K3, turn. BO rem sts.

STRAP With dpn, waste yarn and A, CO 6 sts using invisible (provisional) CO (see Techniques, page 142). With MC, work Row 4 of cable patt as foundation row.
Cable row: P1, C4B, p1.
Row 2: K1, p4, k1.

Row 3: P1, k4, k1. Cont to work cable every 4th row until piece measures 60" (152.5 cm). With yarn threaded on tapestry needle, graft sts to first row of strap using Kitchener st (see Techniques, page 142), and clipping out waste yarn as you go.

Steam block all pieces.

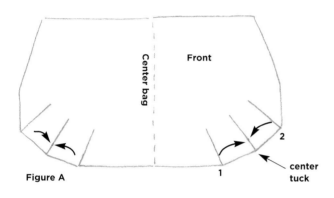

Figure A

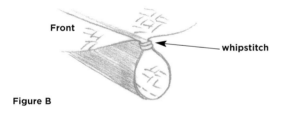

Figure B

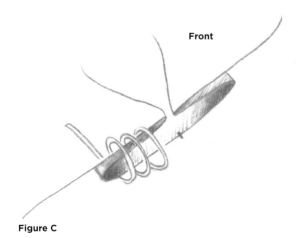

Figure C

ATTACHED I-CORD (see Techniques, page 139) With WS facing, using A and double-pointed needles, CO 3 sts. *Knit 2, sl 1 as if to knit; with right needle, insert into the edge st of flap and pick up a stitch, pass slipped st over newly made stitch, slide sts to other end of dpn*. Repeat from * to *, working around flap curve into every st. Do not work I-cord over turning ridge. With MC, rep attached I-cord instructions along the curved top edge of the bag front (under flap).

FINISHING

Corner tuck folds: (see Figure A) On front bag, place straight pin to mark at first corner away from center bottom (1), then again about 3" (7.5 cm) further (2). Fold and match pin markers, right sides tog. Whipstitch once or twice right at pin markers (see Figure B). Mark center fold of tuck with pin marker; open and flatten tuck to create centered pleat at pin markers. Whipstitch center tuck to existing whipstitch. Open front face of bag and whipstitch edges of tuck to front edge of bag (3 layers of knitted fabric—see Figure C.)

Mark center bottom of bag front and back pieces. Using invisible weaving (see Techniques, page 142) weave one side of strap to sides and bottom curve of front of bag, matching center bottom marks, weave other side of strap to the back side edges and bottom of bag.

I-CORD BUTTONHOLE LOOPS (make 2) With MC and dpn, CO 3 sts and work I-cord (see Techniques, page 142) for 2½" (6.5 cm). With MC threaded on tapestry needle, stitch I-cord to WS of front flap just inside I-cord edge, forming a loop large enough to insert button. Mark front curved edge of bag for button placement and sew on buttons.

Wales

Widely recognized as a part of a traditional Scottish highlander's kilt costume, the *sporran* is a pouch or bag worn at the front waist. The Welsh version is called *ysgrepan*, pronounced "screpan." When the son of a friend of mine was married in traditional Welsh attire, he wore a ysgrepan as part of his regalia. Later, my friend brought me the ysgrepan so that I could examine it for myself. It was made of deep oxblood leather, Welsh goat hair, and horse hair.

While Scottish sporrans may be embellished with elaborate Celtic intertwining designs, the most common Welsh ysgrepan motif is a dragon decoration on the flap. Dragon lore in Wales is abundant, and it's reflected in the Welsh flag, which is a red dragon on a green and white background.

King Arthur is also the subject of many Welsh legends. In one, the magician Merlin dreamed of a fight between a red and a white dragon, in which the red dragon won. The red dragon was thought to represent Arthur's father Uther, so he was subsequently known as Uther Pendragon, the surname meaning "head dragon" or "foremost leader."

I love stories about knights in shining armor, the pageantry of jousting tournaments, and the marvelous costumes, and I viewed an imaginative waist pouch as the exclamation mark to an already beautifully composed ensemble of traditional dress. Building on that concept, I combined several fun techniques into one small Welsh project: the fur stitch, the dragon motif in Fair Isle, an attached I-cord, and tassels that are easy to make. If you don't want to wear this bag at your waist, make a long 3 or 4 stitch I-cord as a shoulder strap. The bag will also look nice displayed on your coffee table beside your stack of books on King Arthur!

Dragon
Ysgrepan

Finished size 6″ (15 cm) deep × 7″ (18 cm) wide.

Yarn Cascade 220 (100% pure new wool, 220 yd [201 m]/100 g). # 8884 claret (MC), #7822 Van Dyke brown (A). 1 hank each color.

Cascade Indulgence (70% superfine alpaca, 30% angora, 246 yd [225 m]/100 g). #10 ecru (B), 1 hank.

Louet Euroflax (100% wetspun linen, 4 ply, 270 yd [247 m]/100 g). #53 caribou (C), 1 hank.

Needles Size 3 (3.25 mm) circular (circ) 24″ (61 cm) long—bag body. Size 2 (2.75 mm) set of 2 double-pointed (dpn)—I-cord. Adjust needle size if necessary to obtain the correct gauge.

Notions Size D/3 (3.25 mm) crochet hook; 1 button 1¼″ (3.2 cm) for embellishment on front flap; long straight sewing pins with colored heads; tapestry needle.

Gauge 24 sts and 32 rows = 4″ (10 cm) in stockinette stitch using (MC).

20 sts = 4″ (10 cm) in fur stitch using (B).

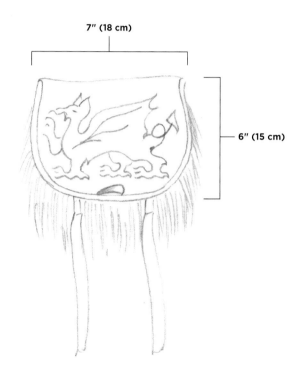

7″ (18 cm)

6″ (15 cm)

Note Fur stitch is quite flexible and it's difficult to get an accurate width measurement. Pull lengthwise and then let piece rest to take shape before measuring.

Stitch Guide
Fur stitch
Row 1 and all wrong side rows: Knit.
Row 2: [K1, make loop as follows: Knit into st, leave on left needle, yarn forward and draw around thumb making a loop about 1½″ (3.8 cm) long, yarn back and knit

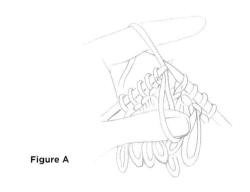

Figure A

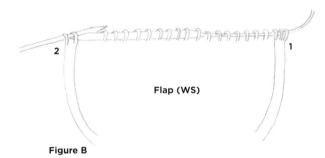

Flap (WS)

2   1

Figure B

into st again, slipping st off left needle. Pass first st made over second and off the end of needle] (see Figure A).

Row 4: K2, [make loop as in Row 2, k1].

Rep above 4 rows for patt. Loops are offset every other row.

NOTE Pull down loop, firmly securing knots while they are still on the needle.

FLAP With MC and circ needle, CO 26 sts. Begin chart with purl 1 foundation row (WS). Work Rows 1–36 following colors as shown. Work cable CO (see Techniques, page 140) at beg of rows with 2 or more extra sts. On

rows with a single increase, work as follows: (RS) K1, work lifted increase (see Techniques, page 143), knit to end of row. On WS rows, p1, work lifted increase, purl to end of row. End chart with WS row, do not turn work, leave working yarn attached, and sts on circ needle.

ATTACHED I-CORD BORDER With WS of flap facing, begin at upper left corner: Using dpn and A, CO 3 sts. Slide sts to other end of needle. [K2, slip 1 as if to knit. Insert right needle under 1 strand on edge of flap, and pick up a stitch, pass slipped st over newly made stitch. Slide sts to other end of needle]. Repeat instructions between [ ], making and attaching I-cord at the same time, all the way around curved edge of flap, and ending at WS of top right corner. The following row places the I-cord sts on the needle tog with the flap sts in preparation for working the turning ridge. Cut A, place these three I-cord sts on circ needle. At upper left corner, WS side facing and with spare empty dpn, lift up 2 "sts" from CO end of I-cord, with MC working yarn purl these 2 sts onto circ needle—41sts (see Figure B), turn. *Next row:* (RS) Slip 1, knit until 3 sts remain (the I-cord sts), k2tog, k1—40 sts.

Turning ridge With MC, [*Row 1:* (WS) Sl 1, knit to end. *Row 2:* Sl 1, purl to end.] Work [ ] 2 times. *Row 5:* Sl 1, knit to end. Turning ridge complete.

BACK OF BAG With MC, work in St st, inc 1 st each end of row every 4th row 3 times as follows: K1, work lifted increase in next st, knit across row until 2 sts remain, lifted inc in next st, k1. Work even on 46 sts until bag back measures 4½" (11.5 cm) from last row of turning ridge. Beg with next row, decrease at beg and end of every other row 3 times as follows: k1, ssk, knit across row until 3 sts remain, k2tog, k1—(40 sts, 6 rows). BO 2 sts at beg of next 4 rows, 3 sts at beg of next 2 rows. BO remaining 26 sts.

FRONT BAG With B and circ needle, CO 26 sts. Work in fur st patt as follows:

Rows 1 and 3: (WS) Knit.

Row 2: *K1, make loop as in fur st patt; rep from * to last st, k1.

Row 4: Cable CO 2 sts, knit 2, make loop, *k1, make loop; rep from * to end.

Row 5: Cable CO 2 sts, knit to end.

Row 6: K1f&b (see Abbreviations, page 146), *make loop, k1; rep from * 14 times, k1f&b in last st—32 sts.

Row 7 and all subsequent odd-numbered rows: Knit.

Rows 8, 10, 12, 14: K1f&b, *make loop, k1; rep from * to last st, k1f&b—40 sts.

Row 16: *K1, make loop; rep from * across row.

Row 18: K2, *make loop, k1; rep from * until 3 sts remain, make loop, k2. Rep rows 15, 16, 17, and 18 until piece measures 4" (10 cm) from beginning. Continue patt as established, with loops offset every other row.

Next row: K2tog at beg and end of row—38 sts. Work 3 rows even. Repeat last 4 rows 2 times—34 sts. Continue until piece measures 6" (15 cm) from beginning, ending RS facing.

I-CORD EDGING Using B, and RS facing, cable CO 3 sts. *K2, ssk (1 st from cord + 1 st from top of bag). Slip 3 sts back to left needle. Rep from * to end of row. BO last row as, sl 1 k2tog, psso. Cut yarn and pull through last st to secure.

FINISHING Using fingers, brush all fringe toward center of bag to keep fringe out of seam. With RS tog, pin front and back of bag together. Do not include turning ridge. Using MC and crochet hook, work slip stitch crochet seam (see Techniques, page 145) to join bag pieces. Remove all pins. Weave in all loose ends to WS of work.

TASSELS For each tassel, cut two 18" (46 cm) pieces of C. With threaded tapestry needle, insert strands at placement on bag front, about 3½" (9 cm) apart and centered. Remove tapestry needle, and tie a square knot at the halfway point of stands, lay ends out east/west. For each tassel cut 16 pieces of C, each 20" (51 cm) long. Lay all strands north/south over the square knot, tie the 18" (46 cm) ends in a square knot over all 20" (51 cm) strands. Fold all strands downward. Cut four 18" (46 cm) strands of C and tassel wrap (see Techniques, page 145) for 1¼" (3.2 cm), using two strands for each shank. Sew button on flap just above I-cord—for embellishment, not for closure.

BELT CASING With MC and circ needle, CO 36 sts. Work St st for 2" (5 cm). BO. Whipstitch (see Techniques, page 145) casing on to bag back, placing upper edge of casing just below turning ridge. Weave in all loose ends to WS.

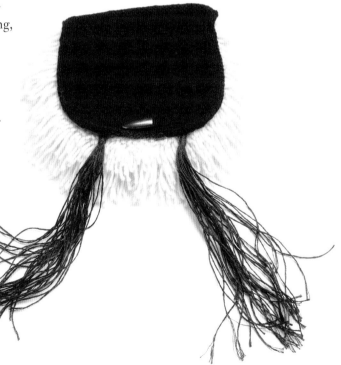

Knit on RS; purl on WS.

■ #8884 claret (MC)

◉ #7822 Van Dyke brown (A)

╲ ssk on RS; ssp on WS.

╱ k2tog on RS; p2tog on WS.

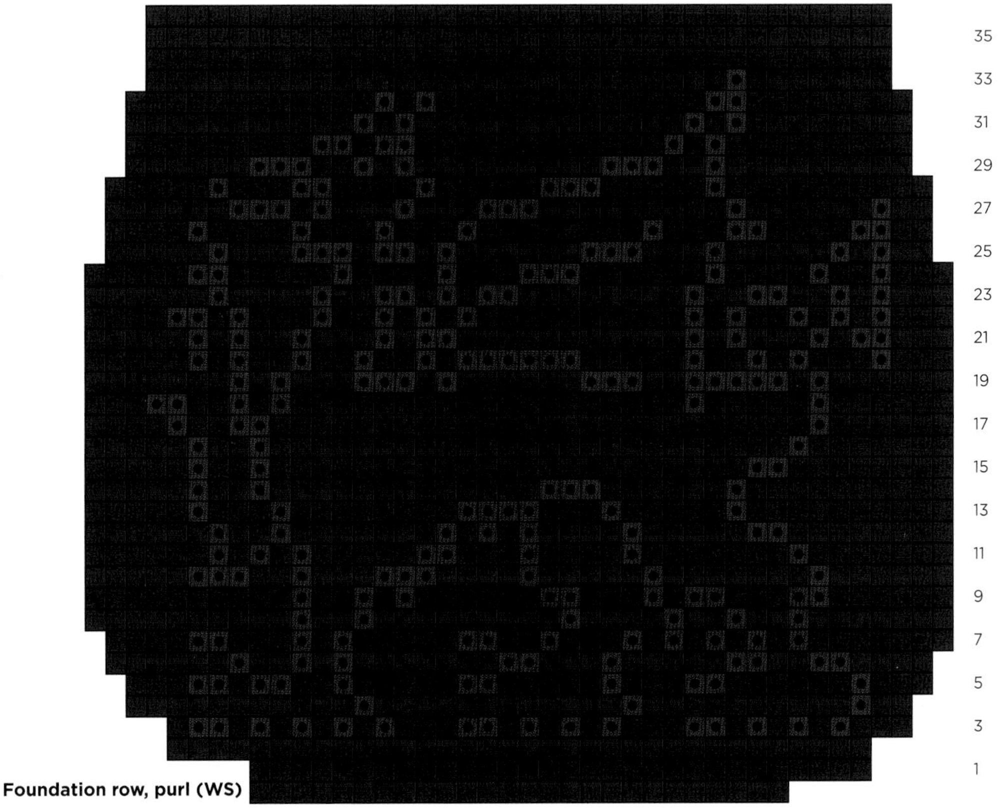

35
33
31
29
27
25
23
21
19
17
15
13
11
9
7
5
3
1

Foundation row, purl (WS)

Work the purl foundation row from left side to right, then beg chart with Row 1 (RS). Work cable CO at beg of rows with 2 or more extra sts as shown. Make lifted increases on rows beg with single extra stitch, refer to instructions for specific placement.

France

Anyone who has visited Continental Europe can tell you that the daily trip to the market is as natural as breathing. There is pleasure in selecting fruit at an open-air stall, buying a freshly baked baguette, and perhaps some cheese, all with the intention of enjoying the repast that very day. Although I have chosen France to represent this concept, I could easily envision my bag originating in Italy or Spain.

I selected linen, wetspun from fine long line flax, for strength, and tested the durability of my bag with a few canned goods, some oranges, and a bunch of bananas. My shoulder may wear out before the bag does! I designed the bag with a knotted mesh stitch to ensure that the openweave structure would maintain its shape. Every two stitches are secured with a stitch passed over, so there is no shifting in the loops and things carried in the bag will not protrude and enlarge the holes. Make the bag and fill it up, it is sturdy enough for quite a load!

Market Bag

Finished size 14″ (35.5 cm) × 14″ (35.5 cm). Strap length: 36″ (91.5 cm).

Yarn Louet Euroflax (100% linen, 4 ply, 279 yd [255 m]/100 g skein). #35 mustard, 2 skeins.

Needles Size 11 (8 mm)—knotted mesh stitch. Size 6 (4 mm)—basketweave stitch. Adjust needle size if necessary to obtain the correct gauge.

Gauge 16 sts and 7 rows = 3″ (7.5 cm), size 6 (4 mm) needles—basketweave stitch. 16 sts and 18 rows = 6″ (15 cm), size 11 (8 mm) needles—knotted mesh stitch.

STITCH GUIDE
Basketweave stitch (even number of sts)

Row 1: Pass right-hand needle behind first st on left needle, knit into back of second st, knit into front of first st, remove both sts made from needle.

Row 2: P1, *purl the second st, then purl the first st*; rep from * to * across row, end p1.

Rep Rows 1 and 2 for patt.

Knotted mesh stitch:

Row 1: (RS) K1, [knit through horizontal strand before next st, k1, pass "made" st over k1]

Row 2: (WS) Purl.

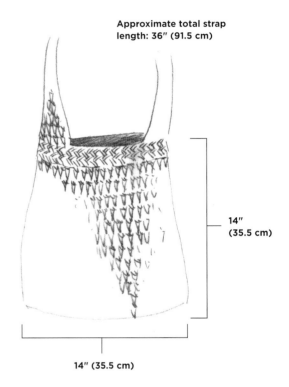

Approximate total strap length: 36″ (91.5 cm)

14″ (35.5 cm)

14″ (35.5 cm)

NOTES

1. Use 2 strands of yarn held together throughout.

2. Pull work snugly down from needle every row or two to enforce tightening of knotted sts and to give mesh optimum appearance.

BAG BODY With smaller needles CO 74 sts.
Foundation row: (WS) K1, p1 rib across row.

Begin band: Work both rows of basketweave patt 3 times, then work row 1 once more—(7 rows).

Next row: (WS) P2tog across row—37 sts.

Next row: (RS) Change to larger needles and work knotted mesh pattern Rows 1 and 2 until piece measures 26" (66 cm) from CO edge, ending by completing a row 1.

Next row: (WS) Using p1f&b (see Abbreviations, page 146), inc in each st across row—74 sts. Work both rows of basketweave patt 3 times. Work row 1 once more. BO in p1, k1 rib across row.

Side seams: Fold bag in half lengthwise; with WS together and 2 strands of yarn threaded on tapestry needle, firmly backstitch seam by sewing together 2 threads from each side at every row designation. Weave in loose ends to WS.

STRAP Working from RS with larger needle, pick up 16 sts centered over side seam. It works best to insert needle under BO edge at each purl st of the rib.

Row 1: (WS) Sl 1, purl to end of row.

Row 2: (RS) Sl 1, *knit through horizontal strand before next st, k1, pass "made" st over k1; rep from * until 1 st remains, k1.

Next row: Sl 1, ssp (see Abbreviations, page 146), purl across row until 3 sts remain, p2tog, p1.

Next row: Rep row 2. Repeat last 2 rows until 8 sts rem on needle. Repeat rows 1 and 2 of knotted mesh patt until strap measures 30" (76 cm) from picked up sts.

Increase row: Sl 1, inc 1 st by working backward loop CO (see Techniques, page 140) on right-hand needle, *knit through horizontal strand before next st, k1, pass "made" st over k1*; rep until 1 st remains, make backward loop inc on right-hand needle, k1.

Next row: Sl 1, purl to end.

Repeat last 2 rows until 16 sts on needle, ending having completed a purl row.

Attach strap to bag: Place RS of strap facing RS of bag with sts centered over the BO edge of other side seam. Working as if you were to do a 3-needle BO, insert right-hand needle into first knit st on left needle (strap sts), insert right-hand needle into purl space near BO edge on bag, knit both tog. Insert right-hand needle into next st on left needle, then into next purl space on bag edge, knit both tog. BO 1 st. Repeat until all sts have been used and connected to bag. Cut yarns and pull end through last st to secure. Weave in ends. Block.

Morocco

Morocco is one of the few places on earth where you can have one foot in the biblical past and the other in the twenty-first century. For almost 500 years, Morocco was closed to outsiders. Today, the rest of the world is discovering—and is amazed by—the skill of the Moroccan artisan.

Nature is the source for the Moroccan color palette, strong saturated shades that capture nature's brief explosions of color. The prevalence of these colors in Moroccan culture is, no doubt, the artisans' reaction to and a compensation for their normally harsh and bleak desert environment. In day to day Moroccan life, the eye is continually rewarded with groupings of bright colors. The oranges, lime greens, yellow ochres, and hot pinks of the long robes known as *djellabas* are juxtaposed with the terracotta of old city walls. Markets are abundant with dates, melons, cucumbers, figs, and enormous quantities of roses. Throughout towns and villages, walls, windows, and doors are painted beautiful shades of emerald green, cobalt blue, burnt umber, and turquoise.

These colors find their expression in the intricate Moroccan mosaics of hand-cut tile known as *zillij*. Islamic tradition forbids any representation of living things, so the art of zillij is one of complex geometrical motifs. Inspired by the captivating designs, I constructed a streamlined bag whose freedom from visual clutter casts the bag's fine details into sharp relief. I focused on a single shape, a simplified squared spiral motif, which I duplicate-stitched in white on a blue background. The elegance of clean, uninterrupted lines is completed with the graceful curve of an inverted Islamic arch.

Colorful
Tiles Bag

**Strap length after
attaching to bag:
36" (91.5 cm)**

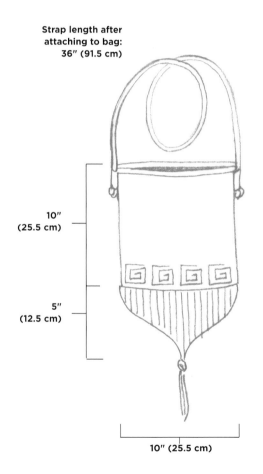

**10"
(25.5 cm)**

**5"
(12.5 cm)**

10" (25.5 cm)

Finished size 10" (25.5 cm) square, 15" (38 cm) deep including lower flap

Yarn Classic Elite Provence (100% mercerized Egyptian cotton, 256 yd [234 m]/125 g). #2631 Kennebunk teal (A), #2616 natural (B), #2657 DeNimes blue (C). 1 hank of each color.

Needles Size 4 (3.5 mm)—bag. Size 4 (3.5 mm) double-pointed (dpn)—I-cord strap.

Adjust needle size if necessary to obtain the correct gauge.

Notions Size E/4 (3.5 mm) crochet hook; tapestry needle, long straight sewing pins with colored heads.

Gauge 22 sts and 30 rows = 4" (10 cm) in Stockinette stitch.

Note Inc 1—use backward loop CO method (See Techniques, page 140).

BAG BODY With A and dpn, CO 4 sts.

NOTE Of the 4 sts, 3 form an I-cord and the 4th is a garter st edge. Work as follows: K4, turn. K1, sl 3 wyif, turn. Work these 2 rows for 10½" (26.5 cm), end with RS facing. K4, then pass first 3 sts over last st and off needle—1 st rem. Cut yarn A, leaving 6" (15 cm) for finishing. Change to B and pull loop of B through st on needle. Pull down very snugly on the yarn A tail to secure the B yarn (and the A stitch should almost disappear). Pick up 59 sts along garter st edge—60 sts total. When picking up sts, insert needle tip under full stitch (2 strands) so garter st is completely covered. Knit 1 row. Change to C and work St st until edge piece measures 11" (28 cm) total, measuring from I-cord edge. BO. With 18" (46 cm) of B threaded on tapestry needle, begin Duplicate st chart working from top to bottom, same as bag body was worked. (Chart looks

upside down relative to finished bag.) Rethread tapestry needle as needed. Make second side to match.

I-CORD STRAP With C and dpn, CO 3 sts. Work I-cord (see Techniques, page 142) for 42" (106.5 cm) or desired length. Work last row as sl 1, k2tog, psso (see Abbreviations, page 146). Cut yarn and pull through rem st to secure. Tie knot in each end of I-cord.

GARTER STITCH SHAPED LOWER FLAP With A, CO 7 sts. Knit 1 row, turn work. Using knitted CO (see Techniques, page 143), CO 3 sts, knit to end of row—10 sts. Knit 1 row. With knitted CO method CO 2 sts, knit to end—12 sts.
Next row: Knit to last st, inc 1 using backward loop CO, k1.
Next row: Wyif, (see Abbreviations, page 146) sl 1 purlwise, take yarn to back, knit to end.

☐ #2616 natural for duplicate st   ■ #2657 DeNimes blue, knit background

Duplicate stitch border   **Lower edge of bag**

4 rem rows to lower edge.

13 12 11 10 9 8 7 6 5 4 3 2 1

NOTE: Turn bag in the same direction as was knit—from top to bottom, and work chart as shown. Row 1 faces toward the open top edge of bag, the last duplicate row (13) is 4 rows from the bottom edge. When duplicate stitching is finished and the bag is put upright, the stitched area is reversed, and will look the same as the photo.

Next row: [Change to B, knit to end.

Next row: Wyif, sl 1 purlwise, knit to end.

Next row: Change to A, *knit across row until 1st rem, inc 1, k1.

Next row: Wyif, sl 1 purlwise, yarn back, knit to end*. Knit 1 row. Wyif, sl 1 purlwise, yarn back, knit to end. Repeat * to * 1 time.]. Repeat instructions between [ ], continuing to inc as indicated every 4th row (every other ridge) and changing colors: A for 6 rows = 3 garter ridges, B for 2 rows = 1 ridge, until 22 sts on needle. End having changed to A and worked an increase row and slipped st row. There are five striped ridges of B of full patt rep from beg and 1 ridge of A following the 5th stripe up to this point. Cont with A: Knit 1 row, turn. Using knitted CO method, CO 2 sts, knit to end.

Next row: Knit 1 row, turn. Using knitted CO method, CO 3 sts, knit to end.

Change to B: Knit 2 rows, do not slip st at beg of second row. This is the sixth stripe of B and marks the halfway point—27 sts. With A: Knit 1 row, turn.

Next Row: BO 3 sts, knit to end of row. Knit 1 row, turn.

Next Row: BO 2 sts, knit to end of row.

Next Row: Knit across row until 3 sts rem, k2tog, k1.

Next Row: Wyif, sl 1 st purlwise, yarn back, knit to end. With B: Knit 1 row.

Next Row: Wyif, sl 1 st purlwise, yarn back, knit to end of row. [With A: Knit across row until 3 sts rem, k2tog, k1.

Next row: Wyif, sl 1 st purlwise, yarn back, knit to end.

Next row: Knit 1 row, turn.

Next Row: Wyif, sl 1 st purlwise, yarn back, knit to end.

Next Row: Knit across until 3 sts rem, k2tog, k1.

Next Row: Wyif, sl 1 st purlwise, yarn back, knit to end. With B: Knit 1 row.

Next row: Wyif slip 1 st purlwise, yarn back, knit to end.] Repeat between [ ] 3 times (24 rows). With A, knit across row until 3 sts rem, k2tog k1.

Next Row: Wyif, sl 1 st purlwise, yarn back, knit to end— 12 sts.

Next Row: Knit to end, turn.

Next row: BO 3 sts, knit to end.

Next Row: Knit to end, turn.

Next Row: BO 2 sts, knit to end.

Next Row: Knit to end, turn. BO rem 7 sts.

FINISHING Place bag body pieces RS tog. Insert garter st lower flap in between bag body (Figure A) along bottom edges. With crochet hook and C, work slip stitch crochet seam (see Techniques, page 145) along bottom edge. Turn bag RS out and weave side seams together using invisible weaving (see Techniques, page 142). Pin each end of strap to bag at side seam with knot placed below 2" (5 cm) mark. Whipstitch (see Techniques, page 145) I-cord strap to sides of bag with A, catching bag and covering seam allowance on the inside of bag. Place whipstitches close together to cover I-cord completely.

TASSEL Using C, cut 6 strands each 12" (30.5 cm) long. Draw 2 strands halfway (6") [15 cm] through at point of striped garter st. Using these strands, tie half of a square knot to hold in place. Position the rem strands centered over the knot, and then tie a full square knot around all 4 strands to secure.

Figure A

Nigeria

A thousand years ago, the state of Ife in Nigeria was the spiritual home of the Yoruba tribe and the center of a great beadmaking industry. Glass acquired from medieval Europe was ground up and melted, and the resulting beads embellished kings' crowns and priests' ritual dress. Beaded caps, beaded walking sticks, and beaded pouches were all part of the priestly costume. The beads on the pouches were often arranged into a stylized mask design, one that also dangled from necklaces worn during the ceremonial dances that honored Yoruba deities.

The purse I present here is a whimsical adaptation of the mask designs found on Yoruba priests' beaded bags. Each garter stitch emulates the rounded look of a bead. The I-cords, the double tube for the mouth, and the shaped nose are all knitted, then sewn on. Finish with French knot and straight stitch embroidery, and you have your own piece of wearable art!

Yoruba
Mask

Yoruba Mask

FINISHED SIZE 8" (20.5 cm) deep × 10" (25.5 cm) wide.

YARN Brown Sheep Prairie Silk (10% silk, 18% mohair, 72% wool, 88 yd [81 m]/50 g). #150 obsidian (A), 2 hanks. #600 real royal (B), #400 ruble red (C), #650 peseta purple (D), #200 treasury turquoise (E). 1 hank of each color.

NEEDLES Size 5 (3.75 mm)—bag body. Size 5 (3.75 mm) set of 2 double-pointed (dpn)—I-cord. Adjust needle size if necessary to obtain the correct gauge.

NOTIONS Tapestry needle; stitch holder.

GAUGE 18 sts and 38 rows = 4" (10 cm) in garter stitch.

BAG BODY With A, CO 45 sts. Knit 10 rows for lower border.
Next Row: Work intarsia as follows: K6 sts A—side border, k33 sts B—center, k6 sts A—side border. Repeat color patt until B measures 6" (15 cm).

Upper border With A, knit 10 rows. BO all sts on WS row. Make second side to match, replacing center color B with E.

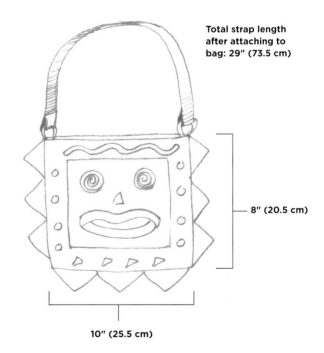

Total strap length after attaching to bag: 29" (73.5 cm)

8" (20.5 cm)

10" (25.5 cm)

MOUTH With dpn and C, CO 3 sts. K1f&b (see Abbreviations, page 146) in each st—6 sts.

Next Row: *K1, yarn forward and sl 1 purlwise, yarn back*; rep from * to * 2 times, turn. Repeat row until piece measures 14" (35.5cm). BO as follows: Sl 1, yarn forward, place st back on left needle (p2tog) 2 times, BO 1 st, p2tog, BO 1 st. Cut yarn and pull through last st to secure.

EYES I-CORD (make 2) With dpn and A, CO 3 sts. Work I-cord (see Techniques, page 142) for 1¼" (3.2 cm). Change to D and continue I-cord until piece measures 8½" (21.5 cm) from CO edge, or until I-cord is long enough to spiral around to make an eye disk of 1¾" (4.5 cm), and there are 2 circles of D around eye center in A.

NOSE With E, CO 7 sts. Purl 1 row.

Next Row: K1, ssk, k1, k2tog, k1. Purl 1 row.

Next Row: K1, sl 1, k2tog, psso (see Abbreviations, page 146), k1. Purl 1 row.

Next Row: Sl 1 st purlwise, k2tog, psso. Cut yarn and pull through last st to secure.

ZIGZAG With dpn and C, CO 3sts. Work I-cord for 9" (23 cm). Finish last row as: Sl 1, k2tog, psso. Cut yarn and pull through last st to secure. Pin each feature for placement (see photo), and using whipstitch st (see Techniques, page 145) sew onto bag front, working stitches from WS.

FRENCH KNOTS (see Techniques, page 141) With 2 strands of E threaded on tapestry needle, make 4 French knots evenly spaced along right border (see photo for placement). Using 2 strands of B, work left border the same.

EMBROIDERED TRIANGLES With 2 strands of D threaded on tapestry needle, and using a long, straight stitch, embroider 4 triangles across the bottom edge of bag. Weave ends in on WS.

KNIT TRIANGLES Make 9 triangles in the following color order: D, C, B, E, D, C, E, D, B. Work as follows: CO 2 sts.

Next Row: Knit.

Increase row: YO, knit to end. Work increase row until 12 sts on needle. Knit 1 row. Place sts on holder. Remove triangles from holder one at a time, placing sts on needle, and working the above color order from left to right.

Next Row: With A, and beg with triangle #9 (B), knit 1 row across all triangle sts to join. BO.

Attach triangles to body: Whipstitch (see Techniques, page 145) triangles to WS of bag front edge, 3 triangles on each side, and 3 across bottom (see photo).

Whipstitch back of bag to back side of triangles along 2 sides and bottom.

I-CORD LOOPS (make 2) With dpn and A, CO 3 sts. With A, work I-cord for 3" (7.5 cm). Insert I-cord through bag front and back at top corners and stitch in place to secure.

STRAP With A, CO 6 sts.

Row 1: Yarn forward, sl 1 st purlwise, yarn back, k5. Rep row 1 until strap measures 32" (81.5 cm). BO. Insert one end of strap into I-cord loop from outside toward inside and fold upwards 1½" (3.8 cm); backstitch (see Techniques, page 139) across strap to secure. Attach other end of strap the same. Weave in all loose ends to WS.

Cameroon

On the inside corner of the Atlantic African coastline, Cameroon is home to about 200 different ethnic groups. The country represents the northern extension of a tradition of raffia weaving that extends throughout central Africa. Raffia weaving was usually done by men, and the cloth produced was so valuable that it served as currency. Raffia cloth also had many ritual uses in marriage ceremonies and funerals. In Cameroon, the vertical raffia loom was used primarily to weave shoulder bags carried by both men and women. Supple as silk, woven from thin strands cut from raffia palm leaves, raffia bags have a long and complicated history. Their forms and design elements indicated a person's ethnic and geographic origin, as well as ranks and titles, membership in secret societies, wealth and status, and even the purpose for which the bags were carried.

I was intrigued by the various shapes that projected three-dimensionally from the flat surface of the boldly striped raffia patterns. Cameroon bags, hats, and clothing all embodied this distinctive sculptural quality. Although I kept the shape simple, I created character for the bag with small flaps, spiral wrapped edging and handles, and a large tassel.

Flaps of
Distinction

Flaps of
Distinction

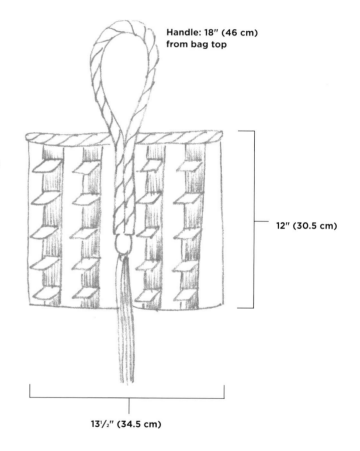

Handle: 18" (46 cm) from bag top

12" (30.5 cm)

13½" (34.5 cm)

FINISHED SIZE 12" (30.5 cm) deep × 13½" (34.5 cm) wide.

YARN Reynolds Saucy (100% mercerized cotton, 185 [169 m]/100 g). #736 taupe (A), #899 black (B), #379 cranberry (C). 2 balls of each color.

NEEDLES Size 4 (3.5 mm) circular (circ), 24" (61 cm) long—bag body. Size 4 (3.5 mm) double-pointed (dpn)—flaps. Adjust needle size if necessary to obtain the correct gauge.

NOTIONS Size E/4 (3.5 mm) crochet hook; tapestry needle; long sewing pins with colored heads.

GAUGE 21 sts and 30 rows = 4" (10 cm) in stockinette stitch.

NOTE Bag is worked side to side.

BAG BODY With A, CO 125 sts, purl 1 foundation row. Working St st, stripe as follows: [10 rows A. 1 row B. 8 rows C. 1 row B]—20 rows. Rep instructions between [ ] 1 time. Work 10 rows A. Work instructions between [ ] 2 times. Work 10 rows A—(100 rows total). BO all sts. Block bag to size, and let dry completely.

FINISHING Fold WS together lengthwise. With A and crochet hook, single crochet (see Techniques, page 144) side seams together. Weave in all loose ends to WS and secure.

FLAPS (worked on one side of bag body) Place top edge of bag toward you and folded bottom edge away from you. Working with B and dpn, pick up 7 sts along a C stripe knit ridge (see Figure A), beginning first flap 10 sts from top edge of bag. Space subsequent flaps 10 sts apart—5 squares. Repeat flaps in each C stripe.

For each square flap: (WS) Knit 1 row. Work 7 rows seed st (see Stitch Guide, page 28). BO. Thread yarn tails on tapestry needle and work in along pick-up row on WS of each square flap.

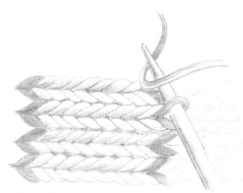

Figure A

TOP ROLL BAND With B, pick up 128 sts evenly spaced around top of bag. Knit in the round for 1¼" (3.2 cm). BO. Allow this band to roll forward naturally, exposing purl sts to RS. Roll should be firm but not too tight. With single strand A, wrap yarn around one end of roll and secure with a knot; then spiral A around the roll, spacing spirals about ½–¾" (1.3–2 cm) apart. At the end of spiral, tie knot in A and weave to inside of roll.

HANDLES (make 2) With B, CO 150 sts. Work St st for 1¼" (3.2 cm). BO. Allow work to roll forward naturally, same as top roll band. With single strand A, wrap yarn around one end of roll and secure with a knot; then spiral A around handle, spacing the spirals same as top roll band. It is helpful to secure one end of handle to ironing board while wrapping. Tie knot at end of spiral, leaving 30" (76 cm) to use later when attaching handle onto bag. Fold handle in half and pin in place, so that the bottom ends of handle are 8" (20.5 cm) down from top of bag, and side by side. Whipstitch (see Techniques, page 145) handle in place from WS. Remove pins.

TASSEL Cut 30 strands of B each 24" (61 cm) long. Cut 2 strands of B, each 12" (30.5 cm) long. Lay all 24" (61 cm) strands over the 12" (30.5 cm) strands at halfway point. Using the 12" (30.5 cm) strands, tie a square knot over the 24" (61 cm) strands to hold them in place. Fold the 24" (61 cm) strands in half, smoothing them downward to form tassel strands. Cut 2 strands of C, each 20" (51 cm) long, and tassel wrap (see Techniques, page 145) the folded strands for 1" (2.5 cm). Sew tassel to the bag with tapestry needle and the strand tails used to tie the square knot.

The Democratic Republic of Congo

The Kuba was a kingdom of the Bushoong people, believed to have been founded in the seventeenth century. Its location was the region of central Africa formerly known as Zaire, and now known as the Democratic Republic of Congo. Regalia such as headdresses, belts, feathers, and beads were very important in Bushoong society, indicating royal descent or other political ranking.

The basic item of Bushoong clothing was a long cloth composed of several flat panels woven of raffia. The cloth was gathered or wrapped around the hips, then allowed to hang to the knee. Both men and women employed a variety of techniques—including embroidery, appliqué, resist-dyeing, and "cut-pile"—to decorate the cloth with angular designs.

Cut-pile is done with an iron needle and a narrow knife. An embroiderer twists a strand of raffia into the needle, inserts the needle between the warp and weft of the pile, then pulls the fiber through, leaving a short tuft with the knife and hand brush. Cut-pile is usually combined with lines of stem stitching to create contrasts of color and texture in repeating geometrics of rectangles, triangles, hooks, and lozenges.

For this totebag I built on the asymmetry of shapes common to Bushoong design. I created irregular diamonds and zigzags, pairing a light natural color with dark charcoal for a dramatic and bold artistic expression. The bag is a substantial size, felted for strength and to prevent knitting needles and any other things from poking out. The glass beads at the top secure the side gusset pleat. When filled, the bag keeps a nice rectangular shape without the beads because the shape is maintained by the slipped stitches at the corners. The double I-cord handles, wrapping under the bottom of the bag, enhance the weight capcaity. All in all, you can really load your stuff into this one!

Bushoong Zigzag

Bushoong Zigzag

FINISHED SIZE About 12″ (30.5 cm) deep × 18″ (46 cm) wide, felted.

YARN Brown Sheep Lamb's Pride Bulky (85% wool, 15% mohair, 125 yd [115 m]/4 oz) #06 deep charcoal (A), 5 skeins. #01 sandy heather (B), 2 skeins.

NEEDLES Size 11 (8 mm) circular (circ), 24″ (61 cm) long. Adjust needle size if necessary to obtain the correct gauge.

NOTIONS 4 round glass beads, 1″ (2.5 cm) in diameter, with large center hole; stitch markers; tapestry needle; clothespin.

GAUGE 24 sts and 24 rows = 7″ (18 cm) before felting.

NOTE Bag is knitted in one piece, plus strap.

BAG BODY, SIDE 1 Using 2-color CO (see Techniques, page 139), CO 82 sts. Work Chart I Rows 1–62. Place stitch markers (m) where shown on chart, and slip m every row. On RS rows, slip 1 st after each m to define bag corners.

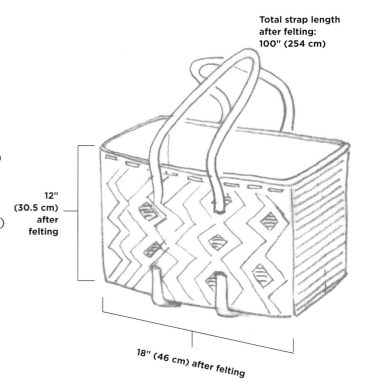

Total strap length after felting: 100″ (254 cm)

12″ (30.5 cm) after felting

18″ (46 cm) after felting

Buttonholes: Make 2 buttonholes on Row 21 and on Row 45 (4 buttonholes in all), as follows. (RS) K8, sl 1, k20, [yarn forward, sl 1, yarn back, sl 1, BO 1, sl 1, BO 1, sl 1, BO 1—(3 sts BO), sl last st worked from right needle to left needle, turn work. With yarn in back, using cable CO method (see Techniques, page 140), CO 4 sts. Turn work. With yarn in back slip first st from left needle to right needle and pass extra CO st over to close buttonhole], k17 sts—(18 sts total after buttonhole is closed); rep instructions between [ ], knit to last 9 sts, sl 1, k8. Do not BO when chart rows are finished. Begin bag bottom.

BAG BOTTOM

Next row: (RS) With A, BO 8 sts, knit to end of row. Turn work. Repeat last row 1 time. Work even in garter st until bottom measures 5" (12.5 cm) from first BO, ending with WS row.

Next row: With RS facing, using cable CO (see Techniques, page 140) method, CO 8 sts; knit the 8 CO sts, knit to end. Repeat last row 1 time. Do not BO; begin bag body, side 2.

BAG BODY, SIDE 2

This side of the bag body is a 180-degree rotation from side 1. Follow Chart II, Rows 1–62, beg with RS row, placing m after first 8 sts and another m before last 9 sts. Sl 1 st after each m on RS rows to define bag corners, same as side 1. Make 2 buttonholes on row 19 and on row 43 (4 buttonholes in all), using same method as side 1 (buttonhole rows are adjusted slightly on this side). After row 62 is finished, work 2-color BO (see Techniques, page 139). With tapestry needle, weave in all loose ends to WS and secure.

HANDLE

With A, CO 7 sts. [Turn work, k4, yarn forward, sl 3 sts purlwise.] Repeat instructions between [ ] until handle measures about 124" (320 cm). Work last row as: K2tog, k1, BO 1 st, k1, BO 1 st, p1, BO 1 st, p2tog, BO 1 st. Cut yarn and thread through last st to secure.

FINISHING On RS, match garter st stripes of gusset sides and seam together with invisible weaving for garter st (see Techniques, page 142). Match center gusset seam to center bottom and whipstitch (see Techniques, page 145) from RS, squaring bottom corners of bag.

Inserting handle: Start at midbottom; bring one end of handle up to the lower buttonhole on one side of bag, insert strap through the buttonhole to WS, and back out to RS at upper buttonhole. Loop handle as shown in bag illustration, then insert strap through next upper buttonhole to WS, then back out to RS through lower buttonhole, and back to center bottom. Repeat threading process on second side of bag with other strap end. Thread yarn on tapestry needle and whipstitch strap ends together.

FELTING (see Techniques, page 141). Felt twice, using the hot wash cycle for additional body. After felting, insert shoeboxes inside the bag to maintain squared corners while drying. Let dry completely. Fold garter st gusset together at top edge, and pinch the fold with a clothespin to hold it temporarily. Stitch folded gusset together at top edge, sewing through the large center holes of 2 glass beads, placing 1 bead on each RS of bag about 2" (5 cm) from corner edges. Remove clothespin, and weave in loose ends to WS to secure. Repeat for second gusset.

Chart I

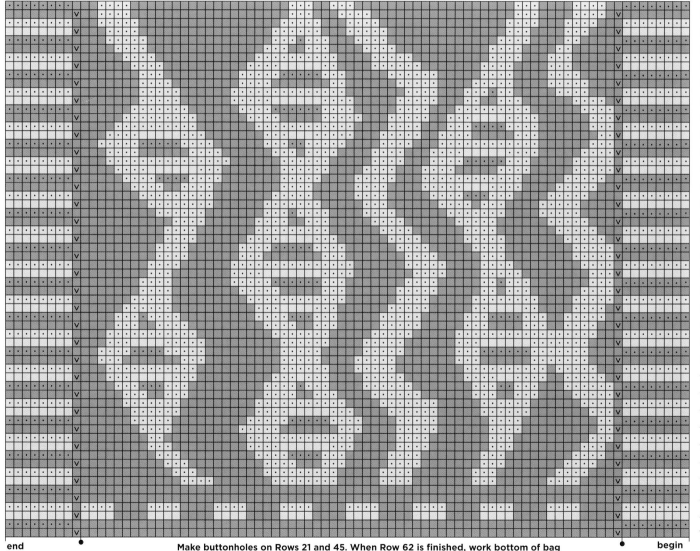

61
59
57
55
53
51
49
47
45
43
41
39
37
35
33
31
29
27
25
23
21
19
17
15
13
11
9
7
5
3
1

end   begin

Make buttonholes on Rows 21 and 45. When Row 62 is finished, work bottom of bag following instructions, then beg Chart II.

Chart II

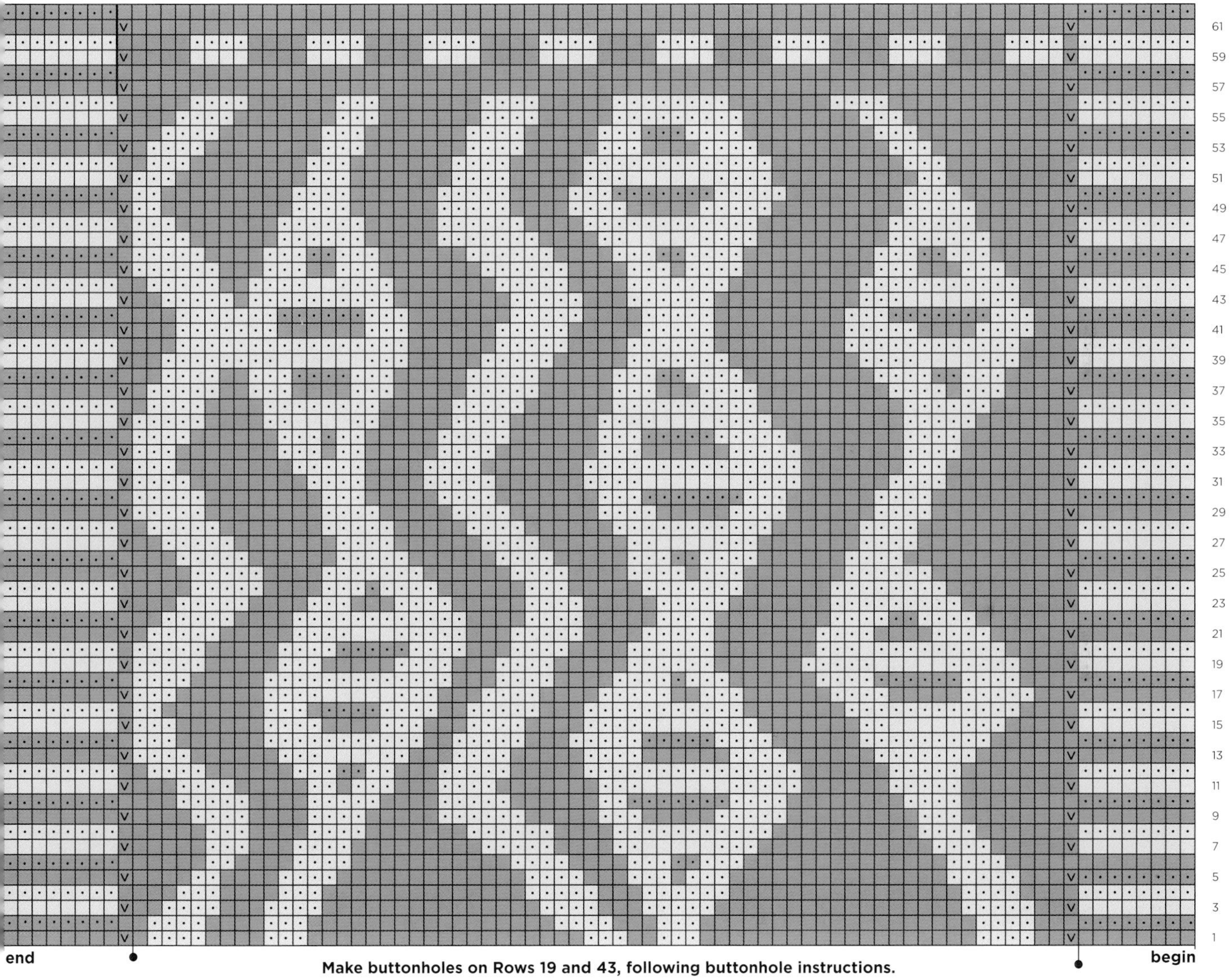

Make buttonholes on Rows 19 and 43, following buttonhole instructions.

end

begin

Bolivia

Bolivia, in the interior of central South America, has tremendous natural barriers to transportation, primarily the rugged terrain of the Andes. Because travel is so difficult, about half the Bolivian population lives in isolation, practicing a rural life that has changed little over the centuries. Farmers, called *campesinos*, tend flocks of llamas much as their ancestors did hundreds of years ago. Many of the women weave textiles or make pottery to earn extra money. Most campesinos live in tiny adobe houses with thatched roofs.

Clearly, the campesinos have a sense of whimsy, as evidenced by their charming doll-shaped bags. The dolls wear traditional historic costume, the male dolls in striped ponchos and the female dolls in full skirts and colorful shawls. Sometimes the clothing is embellished with coins. In designing my bag, I chose to incorporate the geometric images that are so prevalent in Andean knitting: figures, alpacas, zigzags, and stripes. If you like generous amounts of handwork in the finishing, this is the project for you!

Doll
Bag

Doll Bag

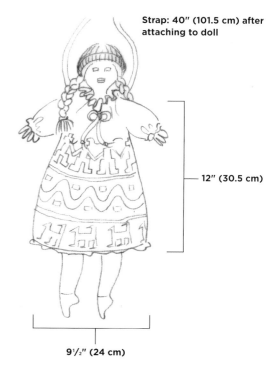

Strap: 40″ (101.5 cm) after attaching to doll

12″ (30.5 cm)

9½″ (24 cm)

FINISHED SIZE 12″ (30.5 cm) deep × 9½″ (24 cm) wide (dress dimensions)

YARN Baabajoe's Wool Pak (pure New Zealand wool, 14 ply, 310 yd [284 m]/hank). #34 royal blue (A), #06 red (B), #37 royal green (C), #15 blaze (D), #35 aubergine (E). 1 hank of each color; these yarn amounts will make more than 1 bag. 50 yd (46 m) or so of a worsted-weight yarn, i.e. Cascade 220, in tan (F)—skin, and 50 yd (46 m) in black (G)—shoes and hair.

NEEDLES Size 8 (5 mm) circular (circ) 16″ (40.5 cm) in length—body. Size 8 (5 mm) set of double-pointed (dpn). Extra set of straight needles, same size or smaller—for holding sts. Size 6 (4 mm) set of dpn—for hat and holding sts. Size 3 (3.25 mm) set of dpn—legs and head.

NOTIONS 1 crochet hook in sizes H/8 (5 mm) and F/6 (4 mm); stitch markers (m); 4 safety pins; small bag of wool fleece or polyester fiberfill to stuff legs and head; long sewing pins with colored heads; tapestry needle.

GAUGE 15 sts and 18 rows = 4″ (10 cm) in stockinette stitch using Baabajoe's yarn and size 8

(5 mm) needle. 20 sts = 4″ (10 cm) in stockinette stitch using worsted-weight yarn and size 3 (3.25 mm) needles, an extremely compact gauge.

DRESS With A, and circ needle, CO 70 sts. Join into circle, keeping CO edge untwisted. Follow Chart I, working Rnds 1–28.

NOTE On Rnd 28, decrease as follows: [K9, k2tog] 6 times, knit remaining 4 sts—64 sts. Do not BO. Begin Chart II working Rnds 1–15. After Chart II is finished, break yarn and slip 30 sts onto an extra straight needle to hold; place 2 sts on safety pin, slip 30 sts on second extra straight needle to hold, and place 2 sts on second safety pin—64 sts. Lay aside.

LEFT SLEEVE With B and size 8 (5 mm) dpn (or size to achieve gauge), CO 20 sts. Divide sts onto 3 needles and join work, keeping CO edge untwisted. Work in St st for

2½" (6.5 cm); break yarn. Divide sleeve sts as follows: Place 2 sts on safety pin to hold for underarm, place 9 sts on each of 2 smaller size spare dpn. Make right sleeve to match, do not cut yarn.

Join sleeves and body: (see Figure A) With working yarn attached to right sleeve, and using short circular needle, knit sts from spare needles as follows: Begin at right back dress and knit across 30 sts of back, knit next 18 sts of left sleeve, knit 30 sts of front dress, knit 18 sts of right sleeve—96 sts on circular needle. Place m. Knit 1 round even.

YOKE

Rnd 1: With B, k2, [ssk, k9, slip next 2 sts at same time as if to knit, knit next st, pass both slipped sts over (dbl dec made), k9, k2tog, k10, k2tog], k11, repeat instructions between [ ], k9—86 sts.

Rnds 2, 4, 6, 8: Knit.

Rnd 3: K2, [ssk, k7, dbl dec, k7, k2tog, k10, k2tog], k10, rep instructions between [ ], k8—76 sts.

Rnd 5: K2, [ssk, k5, dbl dec, k 5, k2tog, k 10, k2tog], k9, rep instructions between [ ], k7—66 sts.

Rnd 7: *K15, [k2tog] 9 times*; rep from * to *—48 sts.

Rnd 9: Work eyelets as follows: [K2, yo, k2tog] 12 times—48 sts.

Rnd 10: Knit. BO all sts.

HAT With A and size 6 (4 mm) dpn (or size to achieve gauge), CO 30 sts. Join sts and work k1, p1 rib in the rnd for 2¾" (7 cm).

Next rnd: Work ssk 15 times—(15 sts rem). Knit 1 rnd even. Cut yarn, thread tail on tapestry needle, and draw through rem loops. Pull yarn to tighten and close top of hat, weave loose ends in on WS and secure.

LEG With F and size 3 (3.25 mm) dpn , CO 18 sts. Divide sts evenly on 3 needles, join sts. Knit all rnds for 1¾" (4.5 cm).

Shape leg:

Next rnd: K2tog, knit to end. Knit 1 rnd even. Repeat last 2 rnds once.

Next 4 rnds: K2tog, knit to end of rnd—(12 sts rem). Knit 4 rnds even. Don't BO sts. Cut yarn.

SHOE Join G and cont with leg sts, knit 2 rnds even.

Rnd 3: Work lifted increase (see Techniques, page 143) in first st, k10, lifted inc in next st—14 sts.

Rnd 4: K1, lifted inc in next st, k10, lifted inc in next st, k 1–16 sts.

Rnd 5: Sl 1, k2tog, psso, k10, ssk, pass this st back to left needle, then pass second st on left needle over first and off end, return remaining st back to right needle—12sts.

Rnds 6 and 9: Knit.

Rnd 7: Sl 1, k2tog, psso (see Abbreviations, page 146), k6, ssk, pass this st back to left needle, then pass second st on left needle over first and drop from needle; return rem st back to right needle—8 sts.

Rnd 8: K1, k2tog, k2, ssk, k1—6 sts.

Rnd 10: K1, k2tog on one needle, ssk, k1 on second needle—4 sts. With needles parallel, cut yarn and graft sts tog using Kitchener stitch (see Techniques, page 142). Make second leg and shoe to match.

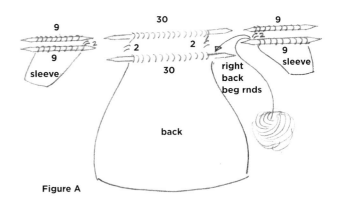

Figure A

HEAD With F worsted-weight yarn and Size 3 (3.25 mm) dpn, CO 14 sts. Divide sts onto 3 needles—5, 4, 5. Join, keeping CO sts untwisted; place m to indicate left side of head. Knit even for 2½" (6.5 cm).

Shaping rnds:

Rnd 1: [K1, lifted inc in next st] 4 times, k6—18 sts.

Rnds 2, 4, 6: Knit. Rearrange sts on needles as needed.

Rnd 3: [K2, lifted inc in next st] 6 times—24 sts.

Rnd 5: [K3, lifted inc in next st] 6 times—30 sts.

Rnd 7: [K4, lifted inc in next st] 6 times—36 sts.

Rnds 8–19: Knit.

Rnd 20: [K1, k2tog] 12 times—24sts.

Rnds 21 and 22: Knit.

Rnd 23: [K2tog]12 times—12sts.

Rnd 24: Knit even. Cut yarn and thread on tapestry needle, draw through rem 12 sts. Weave ends to WS and secure.

RUFFLES With D and larger size crochet hook, begin at side edge of dress skirt; insert hook through lower edge of knitted fabric, draw up a loop—1 loop on hook. With working yarn, yo and draw a loop through the loop on hook—1 loop on hook. *Chain 5, (see Techniques for crochet sts, page 140), skip 1 st along CO edge of skirt, single crochet into next st of CO edge*; repeat from * to * around lower edge of skirt. Finish crochet ruffle by working slip stitch into starting st, cut yarn and draw through last loop to finish. Weave ends to WS. Beg at underarm side, work crochet ruffle around lower edge of each sleeve same as dress. Beg at shoulder, work same crochet ruffle around neck edge.

FINISHING Stuff legs lightly with wool fiber or fiberfill. Thread tapestry needle with F and backstitch (see Techniques, page 139) top of legs closed. Stuff head somewhat more firmly with the fleece or fiberfill, and stuff neck very firmly to avoid "hood ornament syndrome." We want no head flopping about here! Pin legs for placement to WS of lower edge of front dress. Thread F on tapestry needle and whipstitch in place. Pin lower edge of front and back dress together. Working the A knitted edge only, not catching the crochet ruffle, whipstitch lower edge closed with A, stitching through legs for extra security. Work into each stitch, because this is the weight-bearing seam of the bag bottom. Remove all pins.

FINGERS With F worsted yarn and smaller size crochet hook, crochet "fingers" centered on the front edge of the sleeve bottom edge: Work crochet slip st through knitted fabric, [chain 7, single crochet into sleeve edge next to sl st] 2 times, chain 7, slip-stitch to finish off. Weave in ends.

Chart I

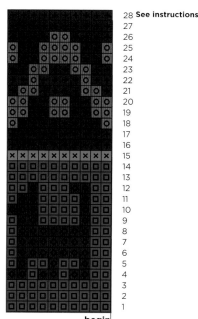

28 **See instructions**
27
26
25
24
23
22
21
20
19
18
17
16
15
14
13
12
11
10
9
8
7
6
5
4
3
2
1

■ **#34 royal blue (A)**

■ **#06 red (B)**

✕ **#37 royal green (C)**

◎ **#15 blaze (D)**

■ **#35 aubergine (E)**

□ **pattern repeat box**

Work 10 st patt 7 times Rnds: knit on RS.

begin

Chart II

Work 8 st patt | begin
8 times

Gather sleeve edge: Thread tapestry needle with 8" (20.5 cm) of B, and catch every other purl loop on WS of sleeve lower edge. Pull yarn to gather knitting, make square knot with yarn ends to secure gathers. Weave in loose ends on WS.

ATTACH HEAD Place head on WS of back yoke, and center it over line of double decreases, with bottom of neck aligned with lower edge of red yoke. Using double strand of F worsted yarn, thread tapestry needle and whipstitch onto WS of garment yoke, stitching along sides and bottom of neck, and keeping sts toward the back side of the neck cylinder.

HAIR Cut 33 strands of G worsted, each 24" (61 cm) long, or enough strands to cover the scalp completely. Strands should lie side by side and be centered from forehead to nape of neck. Backstitch strands on top of head to make a center part and secure hair to head. Separate strands from center part into 2 groups, one at each side of head at "ear" level. With short strand of G for each group, tie strands close to head like a ponytail. Make 2 braids to desired length. With D, tie a bow at ends of braids, cut braid hair ends to even. Place hat on head, and with A threaded on tapestry needle, attach hat to head at front and back with tiny horizontal sts on the WS of hat. Hide ends by inserting threaded tapestry needle through center of stuffed head and out the opposite side. Pull yarn taut and cut. Yarn end will retract inside head.

FACE With single strand of G threaded on tapestry needle, tie a knot in the end of the strand and insert threaded needle from back of head, allowing the knot to lodge in the middle of the fiberfill. Embroider two horizontal stitches for each eye. Insert needle through to back side of head, pull tightly on yarn, remove tapestry needle, and tie another knot in yarn to secure and allow yarn to imbed itself in head. Thread tapestry needle with B, and work same method for lips.

NECK TIE Cut two strands A, each 30" (76 cm) long. Tie overhand knot in ends. Starting at center front, insert both strands in and out of all eyelets, tie in a bow at center front.

STRAP With B and size 8 (5 mm) dpn, CO 3 sts and knit I-cord (see Techniques, page 142) for 42" (106.5 cm). Work last row as sl 1, k2tog, psso. Cut yarn and pull through last st to secure. Tie I-cord onto dress at eyelets at each "shoulder" to form strap.

The century-long reign of the Incas (1438–1532), was short but influential in the cultural history of Peru, and vase paintings from the period provide a vivid glimpse of everyday life during the time. Well-dressed Incan women wore an *unku*, an ankle-length tunic made of two lengths of wide material sewn together, with an opening for the head. The sides were sewn together almost as far as the arms. Along with a narrow belt, every Inca wore a shoulder bag about twelve inches wide, which held food, tools, and perhaps an amulet. Many such bags have been found in Incan graves, well preserved in Peru's desert sands.

The magnificent Incan cloths were embroidered in brilliant colors and featured bold geometric patterns, stylized figures, birds, and animals. My Incan figures reflect the images and colors of these cloths, and the yarn blend of alpaca and wool pays homage to the materials used by Peruvian artisans of the past.

Incan
Figures

Incan Figures

FINISHED SIZE 8″ (20.5 cm) deep × 11″ (28 cm) wide.

YARN Cascade Lana D'Oro (50% superfine alpaca, 50% wool, 110 yd [101 m]/50 g). # 252 navy (A), # 243 magenta (B), #248 granny smith (C), #246 burnt orange (D), #245 cadmium red (E), #241 cobalt blue (F), #250 purple velvet heather (G). 1 hank of each color.

NEEDLES Size 4 (3.5 mm). Adjust needle size if necessary to obtain the correct gauge.

NOTIONS Size D/3 (3.25 mm) crochet hook; tapestry needle.

GAUGE 24 sts and 34 rows = 4″ (10 cm) in stockinette stitch.

BAG FRONT With A, CO 64 sts. Work Chart I in intarsia. BO all sts.

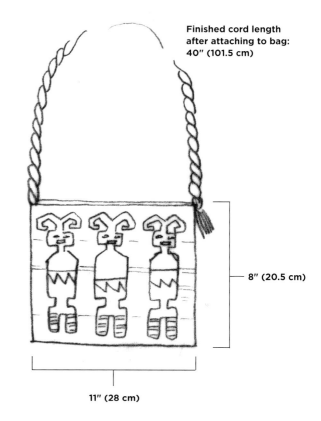

Finished cord length after attaching to bag: 40″ (101.5 cm)

8″ (20.5 cm)

11″ (28 cm)

BAG BACK With A, CO 64 sts. Follow Chart II, working stripes only as shown (no figures). Weave in all loose ends. Block and let dry completely.

With F, single crochet across top edge of each piece, leaving 8–10" (20.5–25.5 cm) yarn tails for later finishing. Place bag WS together and single crochet (see Techniques, page 144) around sides and bottom of bag, working 3 single crochet into each bottom corner to make a smooth turn. Leave these yarn tails for later finishing also.

CORD Cut 6 pieces of F, each 100" (254 cm) long. Tie all strands tog with a slipknot close to one end. Secure this end by pinning it to your ironing board, or some place to stabilize end while you're twisting. With all strands tog and pulled out to tension, twist yarn until it twists back on itself when let slack.

When fully twisted, fold in half and allow it to twist back on itself, creating a cord. Release slipknot from ironing board, and tie ends together to secure cord. Trim the ends even at 1" (2.5 cm). Using yarn tails remaining from single crochet threaded on tapestry needle, secure cord onto bag. Weave ends in on wrong side.

K on RS; p on WS

- #252 navy (A)
- #243 magenta (B)
- #248 granny smith (C)
- #246 burnt orange (D)
- #245 cadmium red (E)
- #241 cobalt blue (F)
- #250 purple velvet heather (G)
- Repeat color patt

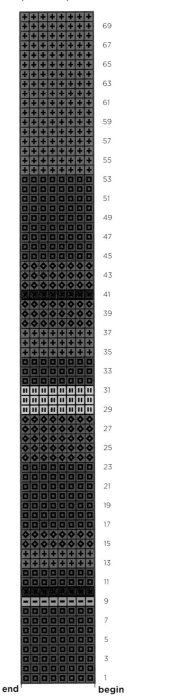

Chart II, color sequence for back.

end   begin

Rep 8 sts between markers 8 times–(64 sts)

Chart I, bag front

69
67
65
63
61
59
57
55
53
51
49
47
45
43
41
39
37
35
33
31
29
27
25
23
21
19
17
15
13
11
9
7
5
3
1

end

begin

Bag front: Work chart as shown, beg at lower right side edge
Bag back: Work chart in background colors only, omitting figures (as
shown in Chart II)

Ecuador

Coastal Ecuador is one of the smallest countries in South America, with the majestic Andes extending from the north to the south. Many of Ecuador's native Indians make their home in the series of high plateaus lying between the mountain ridges. Quichuas are the largest ethnic group by far. Many Quichua villages have their own special product or crop, and the women of Cotopaxi, a northern Andean province, often make bags which they sell at regional markets.

I was absolutely captivated by the exciting designs on their shigras, or "basket bags." *Shigra* is a Quichua word that refers to a special type of bag woven out of *cabuya* fibers. The fibers are worked in a crochet-like stitch with a single sewing needle. This ancient technique may predate the invention of the loom. From the round disc base, women form the cylindrical body of the shigra, alternating rows of natural white hemp with dyed fiber to create designs that are a profusion of fabulous geometric designs, stylized figures, and animal motifs—no two exactly alike.

I was so inspired that I had three shigras done before I came up for air. Mine are knitted in a luxurious blend of llama and wool and then felted. The felting merges the colors into a unified, richly textured whole, and strengthens the bag for usability. I'm sharing them with you in the hope that you, too, "catch the vision!"

Shigras

Shigra Zigzag

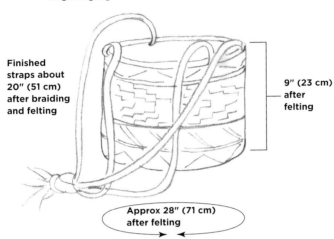

Finished
straps about
20" (51 cm)
after braiding
and felting

9" (23 cm)
after
felting

Approx 28" (71 cm)
after felting

Shigra Diamonds

Shigra Floor Basket

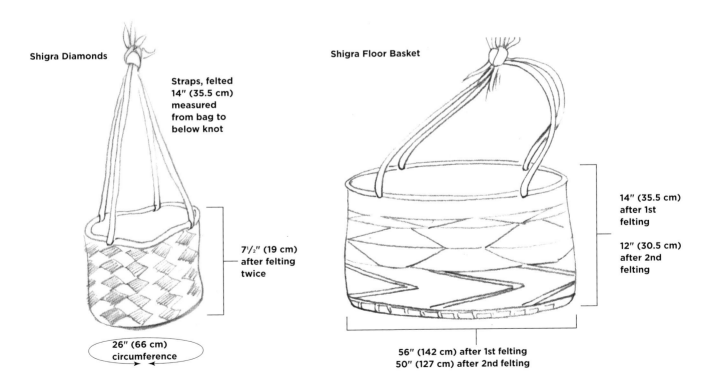

Straps, felted
14" (35.5 cm)
measured
from bag to
below knot

7½" (19 cm)
after felting
twice

26" (66 cm)
circumference

14" (35.5 cm)
after 1st
felting

12" (30.5 cm)
after 2nd
felting

56" (142 cm) after 1st felting
50" (127 cm) after 2nd felting

SHIGRAS

The following materials and instructions apply for all 3 shigras:

YARN Classic Elite Montera (50% llama, 50% wool, 127 yd [116 m]/100 g hanks). See individual instructions for specific yarn amounts.

NEEDLES Size 10½ (6.5 mm) circular (circ) 24" (61 cm) long—bag. Size 10½ (6.5 mm) double-pointed (dpn)—bottom disc. Add size 10½" (6.5 mm) circ 29" (73.5 cm) long for the large floor shigra. Adjust needle size if necessary to obtain the correct gauge.

NOTIONS Size J/10 (6 mm) crochet hook; long straight sewing pins with colored heads; tapestry needle; stitch markers.

GAUGE 14 sts and 17 rows = 4" (10 cm) before felting.

THE KNITTED JOIN The shigras look as if they are worked in the round.

Technically, they are knitted back and forth, because intarsia can be knitted no other way, and they are joined on every knit side row. This is an authentic South American technique used by Andean knitters. To achieve this effect, knit to the last st in a knit row, slip the last stitch as to knit. Then with right needle, lift the st in the row below the first st on left needle, placing it on the left needle and then slipping it to the right needle. Work these two sts together as an ssk. Then turn the work for a purl row. Use this join on the cylindrical portion of the shigra.

Also, note that when you're following the color chart, there will be some stranding to get a color to its next spot. Work the strands in to avoid floats (see Figure A).

SHIGRA ZIGZAG (see above for materials list)
FINISHED SIZE About 28" (71 cm) circumference, 9" (23 cm) deep after felting.

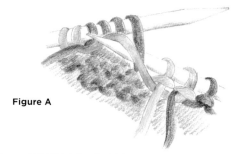

Figure A

YARN #3813 black (A), #3887 pear (B), #3888 magenta (C), #3856 majolica blue (D), #3853 black cherry (E), #3846 maquito teal (F), #3858 cintachi red (G), #3893 ch'ulla blue (H). 1 hank of each color.

With A, C, and circ needle, CO 126 sts using 2-color CO method (see Techniques, page 139). Break off C. Don't turn work. With A, join work into a circle; knit 1 row. Do not twist CO sts. With RS facing, begin Chart Ia and b, working Rows 1–52. Bag body is worked back and forth in St st, using the knitted join (see above) on RS rows. After Row 52, turn work to RS and begin bottom disc.

BOTTOM DISC The disc is worked in the round beginning with the 126 sts on needle. Refer to Chart II, Rnds 1–24 for the color sequence. Use the knitted join method when changing stripe colors to avoid the "jog." Change to dpn when necessary. Work decreases every other round as follows:

Rnd 1: [K12, k2tog] 9 times—(117 sts).
Rnd 3: [K11, k2tog] 9 times—(108 sts).
Rnd 5: [K10, k2tog] 9 times—(99 sts).

Continue to work 1 st less before decreases every other rnd until you have finished

Rnd 23: [K1, k2tog] 9 times—(18 sts). Complete decreases on next rnd as follows:

Rnd 24: [K2tog] 9 times—9 sts rem. Cut yarn and thread on tapestry needle. Draw needle through all remaining loops, pulling yarn tail tightly to draw sts together. Weave in on WS and secure.

BRAIDED HANDLES For each of 4 handles cut six strands: 2 A, 2 H, 2 F, each 80" (203.5 cm) long. Using long sewing pins, mark 4 equally spaced points around the top of bag. Insert a crochet hook at one pin marker just under the CO edge and pull half of the length (40") [101.5 cm] of all 6 strands all the way through. You then have 4 strands of each color to braid until 1½" (3.8 cm) remains. Tie an overhand knot to secure braid. Repeat for each handle. Remove pins.

FELTING (See Techniques, page 141.) To dry, hand press the bottom of the bag flat on a carpeted surface, and fill the cylinder with rolled up towels to allow it to dry with the sides upright. When completely dry, tie all four handles together in overhand knot.

SHIGRA DIAMONDS (see page 120 for materials list)
FINISHED SIZE About 26" (66 cm) circumference, 7½" (19 cm) deep, after felting twice.

YARN #3813 black (A), # 3816 natural (I), 2 hanks each color. #3887 pear (B), #3888 magenta (C), #3858 cintachi red (G), #3893 ch'ulla blue (H), 1 hank each color.

NOTE Only a few yards of B, C, and H are required to make the bottom disc. Therefore, you may opt to knit the disc in A, I, and G stripes. G is used both in the bottom disc and the 2-color CO of bag body.

With circ needle and working the 2-color CO (see Techniques, page 139) in A and G, CO 120 sts. Break off G. Don't turn work. With A, join work, being careful not to twist CO. With RS facing, begin Chart I, working Rows 1–55. Bag body is worked back and forth in St st, and using the knitted join on RS rows. After Row 55 (RS), do not turn work.

BOTTOM DISC The disc is worked in the round, beginning with the 120 sts on needle. Refer to Chart II, Rnds 1–20 for the color sequence. Use the knitted join method on page 120 when you're changing stripe colors to avoid the "jog." Change to dpn when necessary. Work decreases every other rnd as follows:
Rnd 1: [K10, k2tog] 10 times—(110 sts).
Rnd 3: [K9, k2tog] 10 times—(100 sts).
Rnd 5: [K8, k2tog] 10 times—(90 sts).

Continue to work 1 st less before decreases every other rnd until you have completed
Rnd 19: [K1, k2tog] 10 times—20 sts. Work Rnd 20 as [K2tog] 10 times—10 sts. Cut yarn and thread on tapestry needle. Draw through all remaining loops, pulling yarn tails tightly to draw sts together. Weave in on WS and secure.

Using A only, follow instructions for braided handles in Zigzag Shigra on this page. Felt bag (see Techniques, page 141) twice for additional body.

Chart II Shigra Zigzag Color Sequence

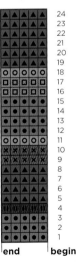

Work color sequence as shown, follow instructions for decrease rnds.

Shigra Zigzag

Bag body: Knit on RS; purl on WS.
Bottom disc rnds: Knit on RS.

▢	#3813 black (A)
+	#3887 pear (B)
✕	#3888 magenta (C)
◉	#3856 majolica blue (D)

◈	#3853 black cherry (E)
●	#3846 maquito teal (F)
▯▯	#3858 cintachi red (G)
▲	#3893 ch'ulla blue (H)

▯ pattern repeat box

Shigra Zigzag Chart Ib

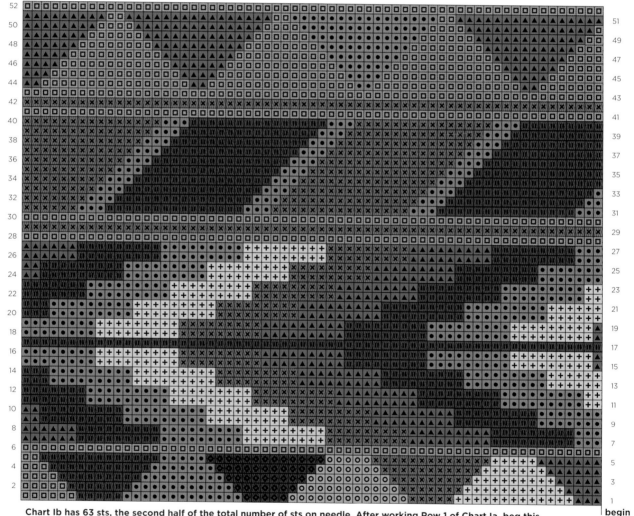

Chart Ib has 63 sts, the second half of the total number of sts on needle. After working Row 1 of Chart Ia, beg this chart at right edge to finish the first RS row.

Begin WS row 2 (purl) on this chart, work to the last st in row, then work Row 2 of Chart Ia. The motif on Rows 44–51 ends with 2 adjoining color H triangles as shown on chart.

Shigra Zigzag Chart Ia

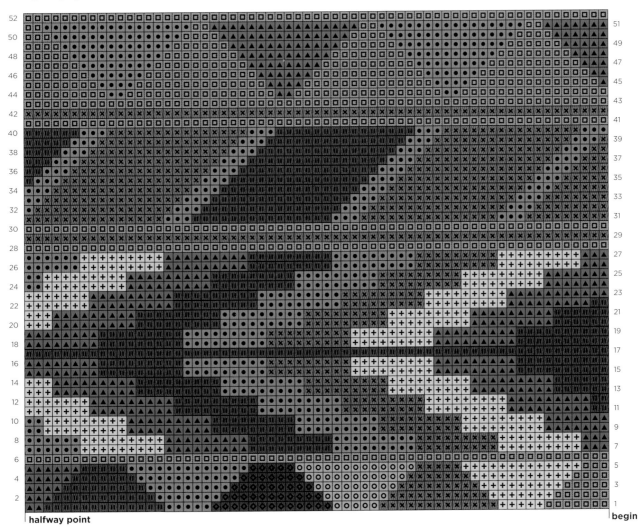

halfway point

begin

Chart Ia has 63 sts, one half of the total number of sts on needle. Beg at right edge with Row 1 (RS), work to halfway point mark, then finish row by working Row 1 on Chart 1b. Join all knit rows together using the knitted join method, see page 120. After Row 52 is finished, do not BO, follow instructions for Bottom Disc. Rows 31–40 begin with 2 adjacent parallelogram shapes in color C separated by color F as shown on chart.

Shigra Diamonds Chart I

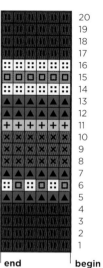

**Shigra Diamonds
Chart II**

20
19
18
17
16
15
14
13
12
11
10
9
8
7
6
5
4
3
2
1

end | begin

**Work color sequence
rnds as shown, follow
instructions for
decrease rnds.**

Shigra Diamonds

Bag body: Knit on RS; purl on WS.
Bottom disc rnds: Knit on RS.

▣ #3813 black (A)

⁙ #3816 natural (I)

✛ #3887 pear (B)

✖ #3888 magenta (C)

▥ #3858 cintachi red (G)

▲ #3893 ch'ulla blue (H)

☐ pattern repeat box

55
53
51
49
47
45
43
41
39
37
35
33
31
29
27
25
23
21
19
17
15
13
11
9
7
5
3
1

end   **Rep 24 sts between markers
5 times**   **begin**

SHIGRA FLOOR BASKET
(see page 120 for materials list)

FINISHED SIZE About 56″ (142 cm) circumference, 14″ (35.5 cm) deep after first felting to make a soft bag; or about 50″ (127 cm) circumference, 12″ (30.5 cm) deep after second felting to make a stiff floor bag.

YARN #3813 black (A), 3 hanks. #3858 cintachi red (G), #3832 puma magenta (J), #3881 lima green (K), #3893 ch'ulla blue (H), #3846 maquito teal (F), #3856 majolica blue (D), #3885 bolsita orange (L), #3888 magenta (C). 1 hank each color.

With longer circ needles (29″) [73.5 cm], CO 240 sts with A and F, using the 2-color CO (see Techniques, page 139). Break off F. With A, join work into a circle, being careful not to twist CO sts. Cont working in the round with A until piece measures 3½″ (9 cm). Work 1 rnd F, then 1 rnd D. Change to St st, working back and forth, using the knitted join (see Shigras, page 120) on RS rows. Begin charts, working Chart I, Rows 1–7; Chart IIa, Rows 1–14; Chart IIb, Rows 1–14; Chart III, 2 Rows; Chart IV, Rows 1–28; Chart V, Rows 1–8. Do not BO sts, begin working bottom disc.

BOTTOM DISC The following rows are knitted in the round, using the knitted join method when changing stripe colors to avoid the "jog." Change to shorter length circ needles, and then to dpn when necessary. Refer to Chart VI for bottom disc color sequence. Work decreases every other round as follows:

Rnd 1: [K22, k2tog] 10 times—(230 sts).
Rnd 3: [K21, k2tog] 10 times—(220 sts).
Rnd 5: [K20, k2tog] 10 times—(210 sts).

Continue to work 1 less st before decreases until you have completed
Rnd 25: [K2tog] 10 times—10 sts remain. Cut yarn and thread on tapestry needle, draw through all remaining loops, pulling yarn tail tightly to draw sts together. Weave in on WS and secure.

BRAIDED HANDLES For each of 4 handles cut 6 lengths, each 120″ (305 cm), two lengths each of A, G, and L. With long sewing pins, mark quarter points at top of bag. Insert a crochet hook at a quarter-point marker just under the CO edge, pull through half the length (60″) [152.5 cm] of all strands. You then have 4 strands of each color to braid as far as possible. Tie an overhand knot at the end of each braid to secure. Repeat for each handle.

FELTING (see Techniques, page 141). When floor basket is completely dry, tie all 4 handles together with an overhand knot.

Shigra Floor Basket

St st: knit on RS; purl on WS, **Rnds:** knit on RS.

- ☐ #3813 black (A)
- ✕ #3888 magenta (C)
- ○ #3856 majolica blue (D)
- ● #3846 maquito teal (F)
- #3858 cintachi red (G)
- ▲ #3893 ch'ulla blue (H)
- #3832 puma magenta (J)
- ◇ #3881 lima green (K)
- ⊞ #3885 bolsita orange (L)
- ☐ pattern repeat box

Shigra Floor Basket Chart I

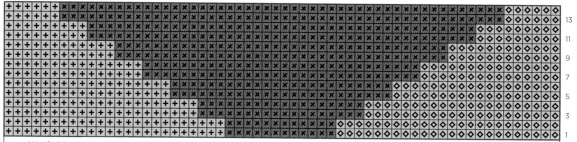

Work 60 st repeat 4 times (240 sts) maintaining upper color in A, and changing lower color with each new repeat as shown below.

Fourth repeat: Third repeat: Second repeat: Work first 60 sts as shown on chart.

Shigra Floor Basket Chart IIa

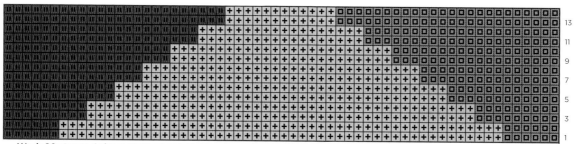

Work 60 st patt 4 times (240 sts), changing colors as shown below. Always beg each new rep with the color on the right, then middle color, then color on left.

Fourth repeat   Third repeat   Second repeat   Work first 60 sts in Row 1 as shown on chart.

Shigra Floor Basket Chart IIb

Work 60 st patt 4 times (240 sts total), changing colors as shown below. Always beg each new rep with the color on the right, then the middle color, then color on left.

Fourth repeat   Third repeat   Second repeat   Work first 60 sts in Row 1 as shown on chart.

Shigra Floor Basket Chart III

Work 20 st patt 12 times (240 sts)

begin

Shigra Floor Basket Chart IV and color sequence

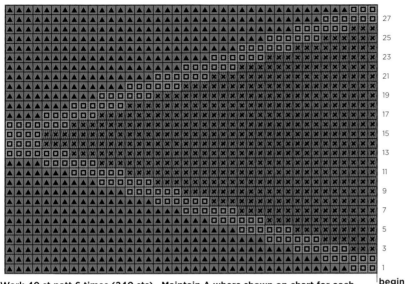

27 25 23 21 19 17 15 13 11 9 7 5 3 1

begin

Work 40 st patt 6 times (240 sts). Maintain A where shown on chart for each repeat, changing other colors as indicated in color sequence graph below. Work Row 1 colors as follows, beg right edge: A, H, A, K, A, J, A, G, A, L, A, C.

Color sequence

end   begin

Shigra Floor Basket Chart V

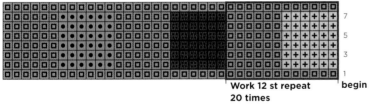

7 5 3 1

Work 12 st repeat   begin
20 times

After Row 1, change colors every 6 sts, first working the chart as shown, then continuing with 6 sts in each of the colors below, beginning at right until all 240 sts in each row are worked. Row 8 is worked same as Row 1.

Color sequence

▣⊙ 12th rep	▣⊙ 4th rep
▣◇ 13th rep	▣◇ 5th rep
▣✖ 14th rep	▣◉ 6th rep
▣✖ 15th rep	▣✖ 7th rep
▣▨ 16th rep	▣▨ 8th rep
▣+ 17th rep	▣+ 9th rep
▣■ 18th rep	▣▨ 10th rep
▣■ 19th rep	▣● 11th rep
▣⊙ 20th rep	

Shigra Floor Basket Chart VI, color sequence for Base

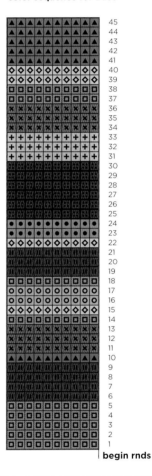

45 44 43 42 41 40 39 38 37 36 35 34 33 32 31 30 29 28 27 26 25 24 23 22 21 20 19 18 17 16 15 14 13 12 11 10 9 8 7 6 5 4 3 2 1

begin rnds

Work as shown for color sequence only, follow instructions for dec.

The brilliant colors of Guatemalan cotton fabrics are achieved through the ikat dyeing process. Ikat dyeing is a resist method whereby a specified number of threads are bundled together and tied tightly at established intervals. When the fabric is immersed in a dye solution, the colorant does not penetrate the wrapped threads. It is common to find these bundles or hanks of dyed fiber in the market where Guatemalan women buy them for the production of cloth on back-strap looms. While it is more common to find ikat-dyed threads on either the warp or the weft of the loom, some weavers use the fiber in both directions, resulting in unusual check or plaid-like patterns.

I have sewn quite a bit with Guatemalan cottons. They are stable fabrics suitable for tops, pants, jackets, bags, and other accessories. I liked the fabric so much that I once cut a piece into narrow strips, tied them together, and used large needles to knit my new "yarn" into a vest!

Obviously, those wonderful cottons were my inspiration for the two bags in this section. The easy-to-make Sizzlin' Stripes is a great project for a new knitter. Spectacular results in color are the reward for using simple, basic techniques in this square bag. The Suede Saddlebag is a two-part bag worn over the shoulder, with the straight edge as the outer edge, and the angled edge as the inner. The multi-colored and solid stripes of yarn pick up on the popular Guatemalan cotton fabrics, while the suede finish of the yarn mimics the feel of leather used to make authentic saddlebags.

Sizzlin' Stripes

Sizzlin' Stripes

FINISHED SIZE 8″ (20.5 cm) deep × 9″ (23 cm) wide.

YARN Tahki Cotton Classic II (100% mercerized cotton, 74 yd [68 m]/50 g hank). #2002 black, #2997 dark red, #2459 hot pink, #2401 orange, #2001 white. 1 hank of each color.

NEEDLES Size 6 (4 mm). Adjust needle size if necessary to obtain the correct gauge.

NOTIONS Size E/4 (3.5 mm) crochet hook; 2 woven leather shank buttons—³/₄″ (2 cm); tapestry needle.

GAUGE 21½ sts and 30 rows = 4″ (10 cm) in stockinette stitch.

BAG BODY (knit side to side) With black, CO 76 sts. Purl 1 foundation row. Working in St st, follow chart Rows 1–61 for color sequence. BO on WS.

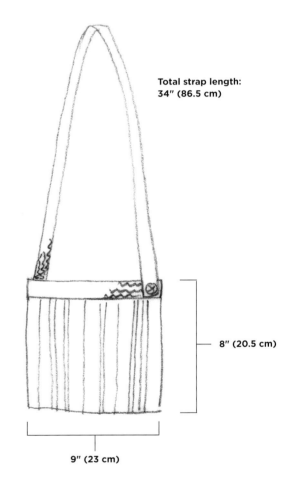

Total strap length: 34″ (86.5 cm)

8″ (20.5 cm)

9″ (23 cm)

61	
59	
57	
55	
53	
51	
49	
47	
45	
43	
41	
39	
37	
35	
33	
31	
29	
27	
25	
23	
21	
19	
17	
15	
13	
11	
9	
7	
5	
3	
1	

begin

Work color rep across 76 sts.

◆ #2002 black

▲ #2997 dark red

◉ #2459 hot pink

‖ #2401 orange

✕ #2001 white

☐ patt repeat box

BORDER Pick up 42 sts along selvedge edge. Knit every row for 1" (2.5 cm). BO on WS. Repeat for second selvedge edge.

STRAP With red, CO 180 sts. Knit every row for 1" (2.5 cm). BO loosely. Weave in all ends and block.

FINISHING Fold piece in half, WS together, matching borders at top edge of bag. With black, single crochet (see Techniques page 144) side seams. Place one end of strap at upper right corner of bag on border. Sew button in place, securing strap and one layer of border. Flip bag over and repeat, keeping strap untwisted (one button is attached to one side, the second button to the other side). Weave in all ends to WS.

Suede
Saddlebag

SIZE 8″ (20.5 cm) deep x 9″ (23 cm) wide pocket, 21″ (53.5 cm) long from center strap.

YARN Muench GGH Safari (78% linen, 22% polyamide, 153 yd [140 m]/50 g ball). #24 terracotta (A), 4 balls. #102 multi (B), 2 balls. #7 purple (C), 2 balls.

NEEDLES Size 3 (3.25 mm) 2 pair 29″ (73.5 cm) circular (circ) used as straight needles will accommodate all the body/strap sts. Size 3 (3.25 cm) double-pointed (dpn)—pocket borders. Adjust needle size if necessary to obtain the correct gauge.

NOTIONS Size D/3 (3.25 mm) crochet hook; 2 woven leather shank buttons—³/₄″ (2 cm)—available at most fabric, craft, and some yarn stores.

GAUGE 20 sts and 28 rows = 4″ (10 cm) in stockinette stitch.

NOTE 2 strands of yarn held together throughout, all colors.

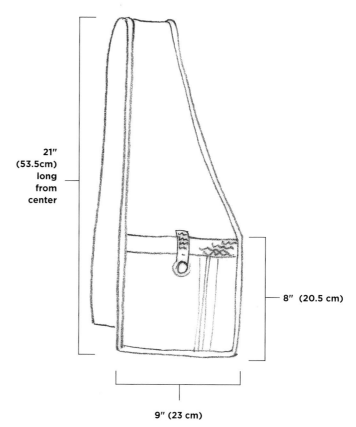

21″ (53.5cm) long from center

8″ (20.5 cm)

9″ (23 cm)

SUEDE SADDLEBAG

SADDLE PIECE With C and circ needle, CO 210 sts, knit 2 rows. Change to (A) and work in St st until piece measures 3½" (9 cm), ending with RS facing.

Saddlebag shaping Work short rows (see Techniques, page 144) as follows: K90, wrap and turn, purl to end of row.
Next row: K87, wrap and turn, purl to end.
Next row: K84, wrap and turn, purl to end. Continue in like manner, reducing by 3 the number of sts to knit before turning, completing shaping with k45, wrap and turn, purl to end. Knit across all sts, working wraps and sts tog as you go.

Short row second side P90, wrap and turn, knit to end.
Next row: P87, wrap and turn, knit to end.
Next row: P84, wrap and turn, knit to end. Cont in same manner, reducing by 3 the number of sts to purl before turning, completing shaping with p45, wrap and turn, knit to end. Purl across all sts, working wraps and sts tog as you go. Change to C, knit 2 rows. BO on WS.

POCKET SQUARE With B, CO 32 sts, work in St st until piece measures 2" (5 cm). Work stripe sequence as follows: 4 rows C, 2 rows B, 2 rows A, 2 rows C. With B, work even until piece measures 8" (20.5 cm). BO. Repeat for second square, matching all stripes.

POCKET BORDERS With C and circ needle, pick up 42 sts along selvedge edge of one pocket square. Knit every row for 1" (2.5 cm). BO on WS. Pick up sts along opposite selvedge edge of second square, work as previous border.

BUTTON TAB AND BUTTON LOOP (make 2) With C and dpn, CO 3 sts. Work I-cord (see Techniques, page 142) for 2¾" (7 cm).
Next row: K1, k2tog, knitted CO (see Techniques, page 143) 3 sts, turn. Knit every row until piece measures 2½" (6.5 cm) from knitted CO. Bind off. Sew end of I-cord to open corner of knitted CO to create button loop.
Weave in ends and block all pieces, let dry completely.

FINISHING Place WS of pocket square onto RS of saddle piece, matching direction of knitting, CO edges and BO edges. With C, begin at upper left corner of pocket square and single crochet (see Techniques, page 144) around sides and bottom, working 3 single crochet in one st at corners. Lightly steam the crochet seam to set. Place button tab on saddle piece approximately 1" (2.5 cm) above upper edge of pocket border and centered from sides. Backstitch in place. On pocket, mark button placement and sew on button. Attach second pocket and button tab the same.

United States

The United States is the quintessential melting pot of world cultures, and artisans of almost all backgrounds use black. Because it's such a universal color, and because the rest of the book is chock-full of colorful bags, I thought it appropriate to design "Your Basic Black Bag" for the United States.

I streamlined the design, kept the shape simple and elegant, and added a few details to keep it fun. I used a yarn with just enough sheen to create a bag that's the perfect cross between casual and dressy. The gauge makes the bag delightfully quick to knit. I designed the strap with two options: Doubling the strap keeps the bag short, but if you pull the strap up while shortening the length between the loops, the bag beomes a long shoulder bag.

So here it is, a final statement of American elegance in black—a bag to go with everything!

Your Basic Black Bag

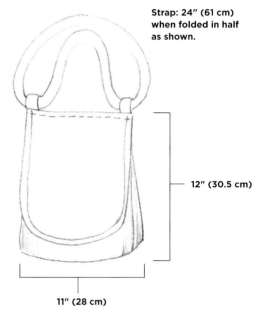

Strap: 24" (61 cm) when folded in half as shown.

12" (30.5 cm)

11" (28 cm)

FINISHED SIZE 12" (30.5 cm) deep × 11" (28 cm) wide.

YARN Muench Horstia Mogador (50% viscose, 50% wool, 99 yd [90 m]/100 g). #8 black, 4 balls.

Size 8 (5 mm)—bag body. Size 8 (5 mm) set of 2 double-pointed (dpn)—attached I-cord. Adjust needle size if necessary to obtain the correct gauge.

NOTIONS Stitch holder; stitch marker; tapestry needle; few yards of smooth waste yarn for invisible (provisional) CO.

GAUGE 16 sts and 22 rows = 4" (10 cm) in stockinette stitch.

BEGIN AT TOP BACK CO 40 sts. Working in St st, inc 1 st each end of row every 2" (5 cm) 4 times—48 sts. When work measures 12½" (31.5 cm) from CO edge, place marker (m) to indicate center bottom of bag. Work even in St st until piece measures 4½" (11.5 cm) from m. Decrease 1 st each end of next row. Rep dec row every 2" (5 cm) 3 times more—40 sts.

FRONT OPENING When work measures 11" (28 cm)

from m, on next RS row, k6, place these 6 sts onto a stitch holder, BO center 28 sts, k6.

Strap loop: (make 2) continue working the 6 sts on needle in St st until piece measures 4" (10 cm) from center BO sts. BO 6 sts. Place the 6 sts from stitch holder onto needle, attach yarn and work in St st for 4" (10 cm). Bind off.

FLAP CO 38 sts. Work in St st, inc 1 st each end of row every 2" (5 cm) 2 times—42 sts. Work even until flap measures 8½" (21.5 cm).

Decrease rows: Dec 1 st each end of every row 8 times, working the knit row decreases as k1, ssk, knit across row to rem 3 sts, k2tog, k1; and working purl row decreases as p1, p2tog, purl across row to rem 3 sts, ssp (see Abbreviations, page 146), p1. BO rem 26 sts.

ATTACHED I-CORD EDGING With dpn, CO 3 sts and knit I-cord (see Techniques, page 139) attaching to flap as follows: Working from WS of flap, beginning at upper left corner, k2, sl 1 knitwise, pick up a stitch from the flap edge, pass slipped st over new st, slide sts to other end of needle. Repeat making and attaching I-cord all the way around curved edge of flap, ending last I-cord row as sl 1, k2tog, psso (see Abbreviations, page 146). Cut yarn and pass through last st to secure. Thread tail onto tapestry needle and weave through center of I-cord. Block pieces.

ASSEMBLE With WS together, fold bag at center bottom. With yarn threaded on tapestry needle, weave side seams together using invisible weaving (see Techniques, page 142).

Top loop extensions: Fold 6 st loop extensions back, WS tog, so that BO edges will be secured when front flap is seamed across the bag top. Place WS of front flap onto RS of front, matching top back and top flap edges. Working from the front, slip stitch crochet seam (see Techniques, page 145) attaching flap to bag and catching both 6 st loops into the seam (Figure A). Turn bag inside out. Fold bag placing side seam over center bottom. Square off corner edges (Figure B), by working backstitch over corner for 1" (2.5 cm).

STRAP With dpn, main yarn and waste yarn CO 3 sts using invisible (provisional) CO (see Techniques, page 142). Turn. With main yarn only, k1f&b (see Abbreviations, page 146) in each st—6 sts. Turn work. Next row: *(K1, yarn forward, slip 1 st purlwise) 3 times, turn work. Repeat from * until piece measures 48" (122 cm). Insert strap into bag through the top side loops as shown in Figure C. Remove waste yarn from CO edge and graft sts to last row of strap (Figure C).

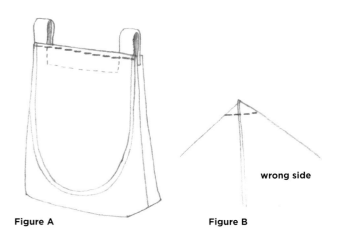

Figure A

Figure B

wrong side

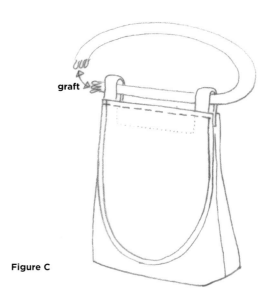

graft

Figure C

Techniques

2-COLOR BIND OFF

Knit 1 st color A, *k 1 st color B, pass right st A over left st B and off end of needle. K 1 st color A, pass B over A and off end.* Rep between** until last loop. Bring cut ends of both colors through last st to secure.

2-COLOR CAST-ON

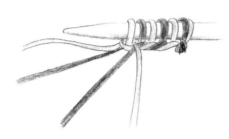

Prepare for long tail method of cast on: Holding two colors yarn together as one, make slipknot, place on needle held in right hand. (This will be worked as 1 st in the next row.) Hold the two strands of color A with tail over the thumb and working yarn over index finger, cast on 1 st. Lay color A down each strand to each outside edge of the color B, bring both strands of color B up through center as shown. Cast on 1 st. Lay color B down to the outside, and bring color A up through center to cast on. Continue to alternate colors until desired number of sts have been cast on. This will require periodic untwisting to avoid tangling.

3-NEEDLE BIND OFF

Place stitches to be joined onto two separate needles. Hold them with right sides of knitting facing together. *Insert a third needle into first stitch on each of the other two needles and knit them together as one stitch. Knit next stitch

on each needle the same way. Pass first stitch over second stitch. Repeat from * until one stitch remains on third needle. Cut yarn and pull tail through last stitch.

ATTACHED I-CORD

Working from wrong side of knitted piece and using double-pointed needles, cast on 3 sts. *Knit 2, slip 1 as if to knit. With right needle, insert into edge of knitted piece and pick up a stitch, pass slipped st over newly made stitch. Slide sts to other end of dp needle. Repeat from *.

BACKSTITCH

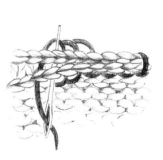

With right sides facing, pin knitted fabric together with edges even. Thread yarn needle and whipstitch edge stitch to secure, then insert needle through both layers two stitches to the left, then one stitch back. Continue working right to left in a circular motion.

BACKWARD LOOP CAST-ON
*Loop working yarn and place it on needle backward so that it doesn't unwind. Repeat from *.

CABLE CAST-ON
Begin with a slipknot and one knitted cast-on stitch if there are no established stitches. Insert right needle between first two stitches on left needle (Figure A). Wrap yarn as if to knit. Draw yarn through to complete stitch (Figure B) and slip this new stitch to left needle as shown (Figure C).

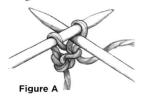

Figure A   **Figure B**

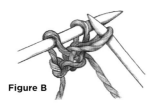

Figure C

CROCHET CHAIN (PROVISIONAL) CAST-ON
Make a crochet chain 4 stitches longer than the number of stitches you need

to cast on. Pick up and knit stitches through back loops of the crochet chain. Pull out the crochet chain to expose live stitches when you're ready to graft.

CROCHET CHAIN (CH)
Make a slipknot and place on hook. *Yarn over hook and draw it through loop of the slipknot. Repeat from * for desired length. To fasten off, cut yarn and draw end through last loop formed.

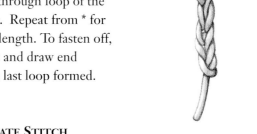

DUPLICATE STITCH
Bring the threaded yarn needle out from the back to front at the base of the V of the knit stitch to be covered. Pass needle in and out under the stitch in the row above it, and back into the base of the same stitch. Move to the next stitch over or down and repeat. Follow chart for desired pattern.

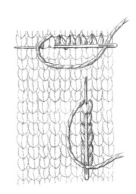

EMBROIDERY

Outline or Stem Stitch: For outlining, bring needle up from WS, then insert it a short distance to the right at an angle and pull through. Keep thread above needle.

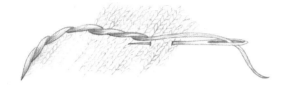

Overlay/Couching: Make a layer of several long straight stitches. Make a second layer at right angles to the first in desired pattern on knitted surface. Couch with small stitches over the resulting intersections to secure desired pattern as shown.

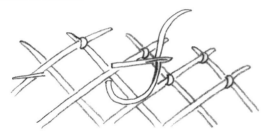

French Knot: Bring needle from wrong side to right side, wrap yarn around needle three times. Insert needle a short distance from where it came out (x) and use thumb to hold in place while pulling needle through wraps to wrong side of work.

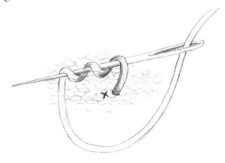

ENLARGING EMBROIDERY

Trace over the drawing, and use the enlargement feature on a copying machine to scale the illustration to the desired size. Trace over the copy onto tissue paper, and place tissue paper with design onto one half of the bag. Insert straight sewing pins ½–1" apart along all the traced lines. Gently lift up the tissue paper and with a water erasable pen, mark the pinholes slowly. Check to make sure water erasable pen dots are visible on the knitted surface. Work from one edge of design to the opposite edge, removing tissue paper as you go. Connect the dots in a smooth line in preparation for the crochet stitch embroidery.

FAIR ISLE

Knit multiple colors by stranding yarns not in use across the back of the work. See expanded discussion in *Knitter's Companion*.

FELTING

To machine felt, put knitted bag in washing machine with a towel and a tennis shoe or a few tennis balls. Let the washer go through a hot wash/cold rinse cycle. Wash twice for extra body. To hand felt, fill a basin with very warm but not scalding water. Add soap to the hot water, mix, than add the knitted bag. Scrub, twist, and agitate the bag for several minutes to get the fibers to mat together. Rinse in cold water. Repeat, adding hot water to soapy basin, and rinse in a fresh basin of cold water until bag is desired size. Roll bag in dry bath towel to remove excess water. Let dry to shape according to pattern instructions.

I-CORD

With dpn, CO the number of sts specified in patt (usually 3 or 4). Do not turn work throughout. *Slide sts to opposite end of needle, knit sts*; rep between ** until desired length. Pull working yarn snugly

across back, connecting last st to first st of next row and forming a continuous cord.

>*I-CORD TIP*: The first stitch of each I-cord row can sometimes be loose and large comparatively. To ensure maximum quality of even tension, knit first stitch, place right index finger on this stitch to stabilize, then knit into second stitch inserting needle fully up to largest diameter of needle. This forces the first stitch to even out.

INTARSIA

Knit blocks of color, twisting working yarns around one another when colors change. See expanded discussion in *The Knitter's Companion*.

INVISIBLE (PROVISIONAL) CAST-ON

Place a loose slipknot on needle held in your right hand. Hold waste yarn next to slipknot and around your left thumb; hold working yarn over your left index finger. *Bring needle forward under waste yarn, over working yarn, grab a loop of working yarn (Figure A), then

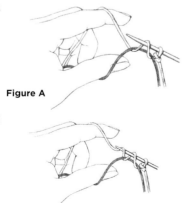

Figure A

Figure B

bring needle to the front, over both yarns, and grab a second loop (Figure B). Repeat from *. When you're ready to work in the opposite direction, pick out waste yarn to expose live stitches.

INVISIBLE WEAVING

Work seam from right side, with pieces to be seamed placed side by side. Note that the edge stitches of stockinette stitch are misshapen: A loose stitch alternates every other row with a tight stitch. At the base of

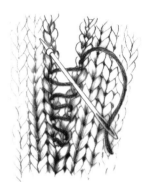

the V of the small, tight stitch is a horizontal bar. Insert a threaded tapestry needle under this bar, first on one side and then under a corresponding bar on the opposite side. Continue alternating from side to side.

INVISIBLE WEAVING FOR GARTER STITCH

Work seam from right side, with pieces to be seamed placed side by side. With threaded tapestry needle, catch the bottom loop of the edge stitch of a knit ridge on one side, and then the top loop of the edge stitch of the knit ridge on the other side. Repeat for length of seam.

This technique is also suitable to use when seaming reverse St st.

KITCHENER STITCH

Step 1: Bring threaded needle through front stitch as if to purl and leave stitch on needle.

Step 2: Bring threaded needle through back stitch as if to knit and leave stitch on needle.

Step 3: Bring threaded needle through the same front stitch as if to knit and slip this stitch off needle. Bring threaded needle through next front stitch as if to purl and leave stitch on needle.

Step 4: Bring threaded needle through first back stitch as if to purl, slip that stitch off, bring needle through next back stitch as if to knit, leave this stitch on needle.

Repeat Steps 3 and 4 until all stitches worked.

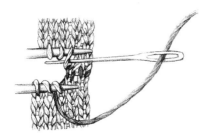

KITCHENER STITCH FOR I-CORD

When I-cord has been knitted desired length, leave sts on needle and do not slide them to the other end, cut yarn leaving a 12–18" tail. Remove crochet chain in waste yarn to reveal 3 live sts working left to right on cast on end, insert threaded tapestry needle through front of left most st, through back of center st, pull through. Move to sts on needle and insert needle through back of left most st, slide off needle, through front of center st, slide off needle, pull through. Move to cast on end, insert needle into front of center st, into back of right most st, pull through. Move to needle sts, insert into front of center st and back of right most st. Finish by inserting into the front of the right most st on the cast on end. Hide ends securely inside I-cord.

KNITTED CAST-ON

Place slipknot on left needle if there are no established stitches. *With right needle, knit into the first stitch (or slipknot) on left needle (Figure A) and place new stitch onto left needle (Figure B). Repeat from *, always knitting into the last stitch made.

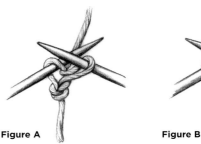

Figure A   **Figure B**

LIFTED INCREASE

Lift up a stitch from row below and place on needle. Knit into this stitch and into the stitch already on needle.

MAKE 1 (M1) INCREASE

Unless otherwise specified, use M1L. Make 1 left (M1L): With left needle tip, lift the strand between last knitted

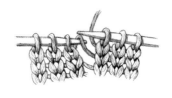

Figure A   **Figure C**

Figure B   **Figure D**

stitch and first stitch on left needle, from front to back (Figure A). Knit the lifted loop through back (Figure B). Makes a left slant. Make 1 right (M1R): With left needle tip, lift the strand between last knitted stitch and first stitch on left needle, from back to front (Figure C). Knit lifted loop through the front (Figure D). Makes a right slant.

ONE-ROW BUTTONHOLE

Work to where you want the buttonhole to be, bring the yarn to the front, slip the next stitch purlwise, and then return the yarn to the back.

1. *Slip the next stitch and then on the right needle, pass the second stitch over the end stitch and drop it off the needle. Repeat from * three times. Slip the last bound-off stitch to the left needle and turn the work.
2. Move the yarn to the back and use the cable cast on to cast on five stitches as follows: *Insert the right needle between the first and second stitches on the left needle, draw up a loop, and place it on the left needle. Repeat from * four times. Turn the work.
3. With the yarn in back, slip the first stitch from the left needle and pass the extra cast-on stitch over it to close the buttonhole. Work to the end of the row.

READING CHARTS

Unless otherwise indicated, read charts from the bottom up. On right-side rows, read charts from right to left. On wrong-side rows, read charts from left to right. When knitting in the round, read charts from right to left for all rows.

SHORT ROW

Work to turn point, slip next stitch purlwise to right needle. Bring yarn to front (Figure A). Slip same stitch back to left needle (Figure B). Turn work and bring yarn in position for next stitch. To hide wraps, work to just before wrapped stitch. Insert right needle from front for knit and from back for purl, under the wrap and into wrapped stitch from bottom up; work them together. Hiding wraps is unnecessary for felted bags.

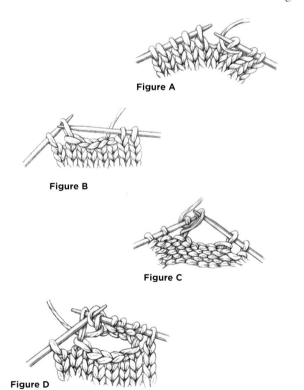

Figure A

Figure B

Figure C

Figure D

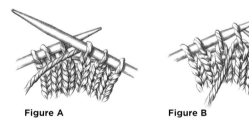

Figure A

Figure B

SINGLE CROCHET

Insert the hook into the edge of the knitted fabric, draw up a loop, then yarn over hook and draw a loop through loop on hook. Working right to left, *insert the hook into the knitted edge, draw a loop through (2 loops on hook), yarn over hook and draw through both loops on hook. Repeat from *.

Figure A

Figure B

SLIP STITCH CROCHET

Make a slipknot and place it on a crochet hook. *Insert hook through both pieces of knitted fabric one stitch in from edge. Yarn over hook and draw loop through fabric and through loop already on hook. Repeat from*.

TASSEL WRAP

Cut a strand of yarn long enough for wrapping. Lay one cut end of the yarn parallel to the tassel yarn, as shown. Fold back creating a loop beyond where you want the wrap to end, and begin wrapping at cut end, placing strands closely to prevent tassel yarn from showing

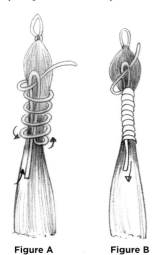

Figure A   **Figure B**

through, snug but not too tight (Figure A). When desired length of wrap is reached, pull second cut end through foundation loop until it lies smoothly, finishing the wrap. Pull on first cut end until foundation loop has been pulled inside wrap to the middle (Figure B). Cut ends of wrap at boundaries of wrap.

TWISTED CORD

Tie all strands together in a slipknot close to one end. Secure this end by pinning it to your ironing board. With all strands together and pulled out to tension, twist yarn (Figure A) until when it twists back on itself. When fully twisted, fold yarn in half and allow it to twist from fold back on itself (Figure B). Release slipknot from ironing board, and tie ends together to secure cord.

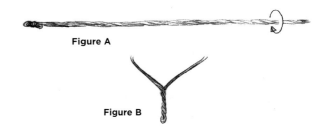

Figure A

Figure B

WHIPSTITCH

Insert needle at right angle through a stitch on one piece of the work, then through a corresponding stitch on the piece to be attached. Pull stitches together, closing both pieces firmly, but not too tightly.

Abbreviations

beg	beginning; begin; begins	RS	right side
bet	between	sl	slip
BO	bind off	sl st	slip st (slip 1 st pwise unless otherwise indicated)
CC	contrast color		
cm	centimeter(s)	ssk	slip 2 sts kwise, one at a time, from the left needle to right needle, insert left needle tip through both front loops and knit together from this position (1 st decrease)
cn	cable needle		
CO	cast on		
dec(s)	decrease; decreases		
dpn	double-pointed needles		
g	gram(s)		
inc	increase; increasing	sssk	slip 3 sts kwise, one at a time, work as above through 3 sts instead of 2 (2 st decrease)
k	knit		
k1f&b	knit into the front and back of same st		
k2tog	knit 2 sts together	ssp	slip 2 sts kwise, one at a time, from left needle to right needle, insert left needle tip through both front loops and transfer both back to left needle in turned position. Working through back loops of both sts, insert right needle from left to right and purl both together.
k3tog	knit 3 sts together		
kwise	knitwise, as if to knit		
LC	left cross		
m	marker(s)		
MC	main color		
mm	millimeters		
M 1	make one	sssp	slip 3 sts kwise, work as above through 3 sts instead of 2. (2 st decrease)
p	purl		
p1f&b	purl into front and back of same st	st(s)	stitch(es)
p2tog	purl 2 sts together	tbl	through back loop
p3tog	purl 3 sts together	tog	together
patt(s)	pattern(s)	WS	wrong side
psso	pass slipped st over	wyib	with yarn in back
p2sso	pass 2 slipped sts over	wyif	with yarn in front
pwise	purlwise, as if to purl	yo	yarn over
RC	right cross	*	repeat starting point
rem	remain; remaining	* *	repeat all instructions between asterisks
rep	repeat(s)	( )	alternate measurements and/or instructions
rev St st	reverse St st		
rnd(s)	round(s)	[ ]	instructions are worked as a group a specified number of times.

Yarn Resources

Baabajoe's Wool Company
PO Box 260604
Lakewood, CO 80226
www.baabajoeswool.com

Brown Sheep Company
100662 County Road 16
Mitchell, NE 69357-9748
(800) 826-9136
www.brownsheep.com

Cascade Yarns, Inc.
1224 Andover Park E.
Tukwila, WA 98188
(800) 548-1048
www.cascadeyarns.com

Classic Elite
300 Jackson Street, Bldg #5
Lowell, MA 01852
(800) 343-0308

JCA, Inc./Reynolds
35 Scales Lane
Townsend, MA 01469-1094
(508) 597-8794

Louet Sales
808 Commerce Park Drive
Ogdenburg, NY 13669
(613) 925-4502
www.louet.com

Mission Falls of Unique Kolours
1428 Oak Lane
Downingtown, PA 19335
(800) 252-3934
www.uniquekolours.com

Muench Yarns, Inc.
(distributor of GGH and
Horstia yarns)
285 Bel Marin Keys Blvd., Unit J
Novato, CA 94949-5763
(415) 883-6375
www.muenchyarns.com

Patons
PO Box 40
Listowel, ON
Canada N4W 3H3
www.patonsyarns.com

Plymouth Yarn Co.
PO Box 28
Bristol, PA 19007
(800) 523-8932
www.plymouthyarn.com

Rowan Yarns (Rowan USA)
4 Townsend West, Unit 8
Nashua, NH 03063
(603) 886-5041
www.rowanyarns.co.uk

Tahki/Stacy Charles
8000 Cooper Avenue, Bldg. 1
Glendale, NY 11385
(800) 338-9276
www.tahkistacycharles.com

Webs
Service Center Road
PO Box 147
Northampton, MA 01061-0147
(800) 367-9327
www.yarn.com

Bibliography

"About Kilims. What is a Kilim?" www.kilim com, 2001–2002.

"About Korea. Korean Traditional Dress: Hanbok." www.clickasia.co.kr, 1998.

Allen, J. Romilly. *Celtic Art in Pagan and Christian Times.* London: Senate, Random House U.K., 1997.

Aschenbrenner, Erich. *Oriental Rugs*, vol. 2, *Persian.* Woodbridge, Suffolk, England: Antique Collectors' Club, 1981.

Cuvi, Pablo. *Crafts of Ecuador.* Quito, Ecuador: Imprenta Marsical, 1994.

Darlington, Rohanna. *Irish Knitting Patterns inspired by Ireland.* London: A & C Black, 1991.

Dickson, Carol Anne, and Mary Ellen C. Des Jarlais. *The Art of Asian Costume.* Manoa, Hawaii: Sponsored by University of Hawaii Art Department, 1989.

Disseldorf, Hans Dietrich. *Daily Life in Ancient Peru.* Translated from the German by Alisa Jaffa. New York: McGraw-Hill, 1967.

Fagg, William. *Yoruba Beadwork, Art of Nigeria.* New York. Rizzoli International, The Pace Gallery, 1980.

Jackson, Paul. *The Encyclopedia of Origami and Papercraft Techniques.* Philadelphia: Running Press, 1991.

Kenneway, Eric. *Origami Paperfolding for Fun.* New York. Gallery Books, W. H. Smith, 1984.

McQuillan, Deirdre. *The Aran Sweater.* Belfast: Appletree Press, 1993.

Minick, Scott, and Jiao Ping. *Arts & Crafts of China.* New York: Thames and Hudson, 1996.

Parsons, R. D. *Oriental Rugs*, vol. 3, *The Carpets of Afghanistan.* Woodbridge, Suffolk, England: Antique Collector's Club, 1983.

Pendergrast, Mick. *Feathers & Fibre, A Survey of Traditional and Contemporary Maori Craft.* Auckland, New Zealand: Penguin Books, 1984.

Sieber, Roy. *African Textiles and Decorative Arts.* New York: Museum of Modern Art, 1972.

Square, Vicki. *The Knitters Companion.* Loveland, Colorado: Interweave Press, 1995.

Stone-Miller, Rebecca. *To Weave for the Sun, Ancient Andean Textiles.* New York: Boston Museum of Fine Arts, Thames & Hudson, 1992.

Thompson, Jon. *Oriental Carpets from the Tents, Cottages and Workshops of Asia.* New York: E. P. Dutton, 1983.

Tzareva, Elena. *Rugs & Carpets from Central Asia.* Leningrad: Aurora Art Publishers, Penguin Books, Allen Lane, 1984.

World Book Encyclopedia. 1989 ed., s.v. "Bolivia," "Ecuador," "Guatemala," "Wales."

World Book Encyclopedia. 2000 ed., s.v. "Nepal," "Tibet."

Ypma, Herbert. *Morocco Modern.* New York: Stewart, Tabori & Chang, 1996.

Index

INDEX